# Training Horses
*the* Ingrid Klimke Way

Other books and DVDs by Ingrid Klimke:

*Cavalletti* (Book)

*Basic Training of the Young Horse* (Book)

*Basic Training for Riding Horses* (DVDs)

*Success through Cavalletti-Training* (DVD)

*Training for Dressage Horses* (DVDs)

*Just Paul: The Making of a Dressage Horse* (DVD)

# Training Horses
## *the* Ingrid Klimke Way

An Olympic Medalist's Winning Methods
for a Joyful Riding Partnership

## INGRID KLIMKE
### Translated by Karen Brittle

TRAFALGAR SQUARE
North Pomfret, Vermont

First published in the United States of America in 2017 by

Trafalgar Square Books
North Pomfret, Vermont  05053

Originally published in the German language as *Reite zu Deiner Freude* by Franckh-Kosmos Verlags-GmbH & Co. KG, Stuttgart

Copyright © 2016 Franckh-Kosmos Verlags

English translation © 2017 Trafalgar Square Books

**Disclaimer of Liability**

The author and publisher shall have neither liability nor responsibility to any person or entity with respect to any loss or damage caused or alleged to be caused directly or indirectly by the information contained in this book. While the book is as accurate as the author can make it, there may be errors, omissions, and inaccuracies.

Trafalgar Square Books encourages the use of approved riding helmets in all equestrian sports and activities.

Library of Congress Control Number: 2017931627

All photographs by Horst Streitferdt except:  Carina Bein (p. 146); Gabriele Boiselle (p. 50 bottom); Hanna Broms (p. 26); Arnd Bronkhorst (p. 46 left); Werner Ernst (pp. v, 45 right); Klaus Jürgen Guni (p. 170 bottom right); Roland Hogrebe (p. 159); Trevor Holt (p. 156); Libby Law (p. 139); Maren Leichhauer/Kosmos (p. 42 top); L-L-Foto (pp. 9, 35, 71, 149); Julia Rau/Kosmos (pp. 16 bottom, 37 top, 97, 102, 104, 105, 151, 158; Julia Rau (pp. 17, 19, 21, 39 left, 43, 45 bottom, 46 right, 135, 154, 155, 157; Barbara Schnell (p. 127); Inge Vogel (pp. ix, 38, 39 right, 41, 57, 68, 75, 92, 96, 147, 148); Ingo Wächter (p. 40)

Illustrations by Cornelia Koller and Atelier Krohmer

Interior design by Peter Schmidt Group GmbH, Hamburg

Cover design by RM Didier

Printed in China

10 9 8 7 6 5 4 3 2 1

# FOR MY FATHER

*A love of horses and the art of riding were laid forth for me by my father.*

*I often think of him and all I learned from him.*

*Dr. Reiner Klimke on Ahlerich.*

# ☞ *Contents*

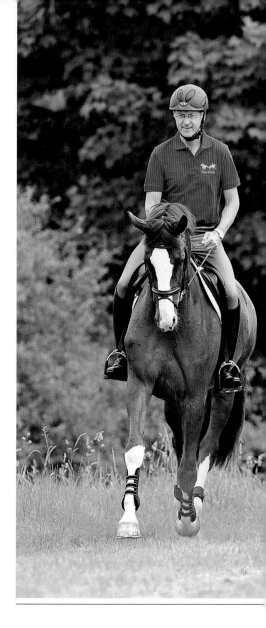

# FOREWORD:
# PRESERVING TRADITION

As a highly successful rider, Dr. Reiner Klimke combined theoretical knowledge and riding ability in a very rare way. He passed this exceptional ability along to his daughter Ingrid—along with the tradition of regarding the horse as a family member and partner, and providing the horse with both a versatile education and a way of life that considers the needs of his species. Ingrid has made good on living these values and passing them along to the next generation. It is important to observe the proven fundamentals when interacting with and training the horse, and to keep these traditions alive. This is the only correct way. Because this riding methodology—in particular, that reflected in the *H.Dv.12 German Cavalry Manual*—has been preserved and passed on, we have a solid horsemanship foundation in Germany of which we can be proud.

I'm so pleased Ingrid has proved so worthy of furthering her father's legacy—an admirable role model and certified German Riding Master, as well as a successful dressage and event rider, she continuously updated Dr. Klimke's riding theory, recorded in his books. And now the time has come for Ingrid to write her own book about her life with horses. To begin, she provides the reader with the guiding principles of her training methods, allowing insight into her horses and their training. Her methods include much from the traditions of her father, now with her own personal touch. He would be proud of his daughter and what she has achieved so far in her riding life, as well as how she has navigated her own way in the wake of her father's impressive example.

I feel personally connected with the Klimke family; we share the same understanding about how horses should be ridden. With pleasure, I can assure all that Ingrid rides using the traditional fundamentals of classical training, as described in this book, and that she faithfully passes these principles along to her students and to many young riders. This is an important task, as it means that the tradition of exemplary riding will continue. I have dedicated my entire life to this purpose, and I know in my heart that Ingrid will do so also, helping to ensure coming generations will be taught horsemanship in a way that is serious, in-depth, and respectful.

**PAUL STECKEN**

Major a.D. Paul Stecken was born June 29, 1916, in Munster, Germany. He received his fundamental and formative education as a rider through the cavalry regiment. Therefore, in all his years as a trainer, he made sure to educate horses and riders in adherence with the regulations put forth in the German Cavalry Manual. In 1950, he took over for his father, Heinrich Stecken, as the director of the Westphalian School for Riding and Driving. In this role, Paul Stecken worked formatively on the education of riders in Germany until 1985. He encouraged and supported Dr. Reiner Klimke in the training of his horses and also taught Ingrid Klimke.

**PAUL STECKEN**
Major a.D., Director of the Westphalian School
for Riding and Driving, 1950–1985

# PREFACE: RIDING FOR JOY

For many years now, I've considered writing a book about my work and my life with horses. But there are only 24 hours in a day and with the training and education of my horses, the instruction of my students, the competitions, championships, clinics, seminars, and precious time spent with my family, I am more than busy. And time just flies by! With each year, as I gain experiences, score victories, survive defeat, experience much joy and sometimes doubts, it becomes clearer and clearer to me how truly fortunate I am. I have been able to occupy my life with the most wonderful tasks I can imagine: the education, training, and competition of horses. For this, I'm extremely thankful and remind myself almost every day of this gift.

So, my desire to give back grew. I don't only want to show my appreciation and recognition to the horses that carry me or the people who support me. I would like to have an effect on all horses and friends of horses. In part, I can accomplish this through clinics or by regularly offering "Open Training" at my barn, or even with my ongoing intention to always be a good role model for today's riders. But I can also have an effect by writing down my experiences, introducing you to the horses I get to spend my time with, and explaining my training philosophy.

This book is the result of my riding life up to this point. It has its origins in the thoughts and actions of my father, Dr. Reiner Klimke. He worked tirelessly for better, more horse-centered riding. I want to continue to travel this path, and with my own experiences, enrich it. I also want to describe all I learned and inherited from him, as well as how other important horse people inspired, and how they guided me in my development up to this point. This book is not a riding guide and does not attempt to describe step-by-step the systematic training of a riding horse through the levels. It is much more important to me to use examples that will impart the joy of riding, and a rich, diversified approach to daily training.

An important event in my career path as a rider was my appointment to Riding Master by the German Equestrian Federation in 2012. It was such an honor to take on this title. I am,

*Enjoying some downtime after work is done.*

*"Ride for joy"—My father passed this saying down to me, somewhere along the way.*

however, also conscious of the major responsibility that comes with it. I want to do justice to the title. Therefore, I train further, question myself, consider the views of others, and remain open to all riding styles. Anyone who cares to be a good rider must first of all work on herself: on her inner bearing, her general attitude toward horses, her physical readiness (of course), and on giving aids clearly and "with feel" for the horse.

My approach to training complies with classical German training principles. After the death of my father, my mentor along this path became Paul Stecken, one of the last major representatives of the old cavalry riding school. In recent years, I have been majorly influenced by Paul's immense knowledge, unshakeable commitment to the conscientious training of horses, and his ability to always see the best in them. In the pages that follow, I would like to share with you the knowledge my father, Paul, and still others have given me, along with my own insights. Of course, the most important characters are always the horses. These cooperative animals deserve for us to listen to them and to work together with them—respectfully and in partnership.

I hope my thoughts will help you toward a better understanding with your horse, as well as a harmonious partnership and joyfulness whenever you are together.

You can find all important information about Ingrid Klimke and her horses on her homepage: **www.ingrid-klimke.de**

Ingrid Klimke

*The good fairy watched over it all.*

# My Guiding Principles
## — For Training

# Fundamentals

*My father's most important message: the horse is the rider's partner, not a piece of sporting equipment! Treat the horse as you would your best friend.*

## Training Your Own Young Horses

One of my father's fundamental beliefs was to train his horses himself, not to buy horses that had already been completely finished. He had trained practically every one of his successful horses under saddle from the beginning, and this was the secret to their mutual success. With his best horse, Ahlerich, he would never have got as far as he did had he not established a relationship full of trust from the beginning. This relationship was sustainably formed by taking the necessary time to develop a deep connection. Ali was a very sensitive, intelligent, and strong-willed horse who required much from his rider. He was only prepared to give his outstanding performance when his outer and inner conditions were in tune. For this, human and horse need trust and understanding for one another. These are not things that you obtain overnight. Rather, they must grow and require ongoing care.

*Dressage in an open field provides variety in the training plan.*

*Going bravely through the puddle: young horses build trust in their rider through positive experience.*

I've had the same experiences with my horses. Ideally, I train them from the beginning myself, so that they can develop a wholesome, essential trust in me and for my riding style. I ride as appropriate for their age, and make sure to provide a training program with lots of variety, including longeing over cavalletti, mounted cavalletti work, riding out in a group, conditioning and gymnastic work on hills, and gymnastic jumping as well as dressage, in-hand work, and work with long-lines. They are turned out daily and get the social contact they need. And they are given the time they need to develop well. In this way, I get to know the individual personalities of the young horses early on and can also then ride them much better based on this knowledge of their individual characteristics. I respect and empower their personalities. Only then will they develop sufficient confidence in their own ability.

This doesn't mean that I allow my horses to do whatever they want. Quite the opposite! I give them a clear, definite command and show them the way. They learn to trust me. This gives them security. Certainly, I must always make sure they understand my request and are situated so as to be able to execute what I've asked. If a horse is asked to do a task that he can't complete, either because he hasn't understood or he's not physically capable of completing it, this means stress. It's imperative to avoid stress when training horses. I want to win over the horse's cooperation, motivate him, and prepare him well for his tasks. As soon as I get the feeling that a horse is losing his willingness, is not feeling well physically, is becoming weak or inattentive, I respond accordingly. With young horses, it can often happen that they go through a growth spurt and become so preoccupied with their own body that they don't feel well when ridden. In cases like these, we just get the horse moving lightly until I have the feeling that we can resume more vigorous work with this horse.

My father always said, "Good horses are made." I agree with him. My event horse, Horseware Hale Bob OLD, is the best example of this. Over and over, I was asked what I saw in this horse. Most people found him very average and, in fact, he was unremarkable when he first came to me. However, he improved from year to year. Eventually, it was Bobby with whom I won my first Four Star (CCI****) event in 2014, achieved second place at the Four Star event in Badminton in 2015, and then was able to win Team Gold at the European Championships at Blair Castle. In 2015, he was the most successful event horse in the world. A few years earlier, no one would have credited him with this amazing ability, and I also had had doubts for a long time about whether we could get that far.

*Horseware Hale Bob OLD at the 2015 Three Star event in Aachen, where we won second place.*

*My dressage horse Franziskus jumps with enthusiasm.*

## Versatile Basic Training

It's very important to me that all my horses experience a fundamental education that is rich in variety and emphasizes versatility, no matter what they will specialize in later — dressage, show jumping, or eventing. Specializing too early harms the horse physically and mentally.

When a young horse is only ridden in one way, he does not develop balanced musculature. In this case, too much is demanded of some muscle groups, which damages the still-growing body. With a versatile basic training plan that includes riding out in the open, work with cavalletti and gymnastic jumping, the demand on muscles, tendons, and joints is more evenly distributed. The horse will be evenly "gymnasticized." Instead of overly stressing individual body parts, the goal is to deliberately build up the overall muscling the horse needs. The horse learns to go on different terrain, develop his sense of balance, and become familiar with a variety of sensory stimuli, which all help to cultivate relaxation and strengthen his courage.

All my young horses are trained in this way. Only after they have this fundamental education behind them will they be trained in a specific discipline, which does not mean that the rich variety of gymnastic

*Water in the riding ring can add a welcome variety.*

activities becomes any less. In order for the young horse to develop well, he must draw from many positive experiences. Here, too, I achieve optimal results when I ensure variety in the training. So, I quickly discover where my young horse is especially talented, and which tasks he enjoys learning. This allows me to facilitate a targeted sense of achievement for this horse.

A young horse should always be trained in accordance with the Training Scale. This means: rhythm, relaxed suppleness, contact, impulsion, straightness and collection must be developed, step by step. As this takes place, these individual concepts overlap with one another, mutually influencing one another, and cannot be developed in isolation from one another.

From the beginning on, I work on balance and *durchlässigkeit*,

*Dressage training in an open field schools the young horse in a variety of ways. Sure-footedness and concentration are developed, while I get movement with impulsion as a "gift" thanks to the new environment.*

which means willing cooperation on the part of the horse to accept my aids and allow the aids "through" his body. Each stage of training must be diligently carried out and solidified before the next stage can be introduced. Otherwise, I'm missing the fundamentals from which to build. Or, as Paul Stecken would say, "At some point, the horse will be far up the ladder but unfortunately a few rungs will be missing." Over the long run, this cannot go well. At the latest, this horse will start having problems when we approach movements involving collection.

With finished horses that I acquire, I never know how the foundational training went off. This is yet another reason I prefer to start my horses myself, from the beginning. In my book *Basic Training of the Young Horse,* you can read in detail about how to correctly train your young horse from backing through age six.

# Versatility Training for the Body

Just like the horse, the rider's training also needs to incorporate variety. Back when my father competed, dressage tests incorporated a small jump to test obedience. This jump was part of the test and, because it was very low, it did not pose a problem for the rider or the horse. But, it set the expectation that both dressage riders and dressage horses should be able to negotiate a small jump. Today, unfortunately, this jump to test obedience is no longer included and, therefore, many dressage riders never experience the sense of elation from jumping over a small fence.

In my mind, it's significant that these riders also miss out on one of the most important building blocks of their physical training. Every good rider needs to be balanced and have a seat that is independent from her hands. This is an essential part of knowing how to ride. When a rider plays early on with small jumps or cavalletti without any pressure, as I did in my youth and as my daughters do now, the rider automatically develops good body awareness and a balanced seat. The same goes for gaining experience by riding out on trails or galloping on a track. My father had a galloping track around his dressage arena and used it to loosen up his horses, as well as to work on straight lines. It was a given that the rider was simultaneously training her body awareness. We didn't even think about this — it just was. In and of themselves, the various stirrup lengths needed for schooling in dressage, jumping, or riding cross-country provide the rider with various physical experiences, which lead to the development of a balanced, secure, and relaxed seat.

# Gaining Knowledge

Paul Stecken always says, "You must first understand what you're riding — in your mind."

I can really only execute an exercise properly when I fully understand the theory — why and how I am riding the exercise to begin with. For this, I need the relevant knowledge, which is either imparted to me by my riding instructor, or which I gain by reading books, listening to special lectures, watching DVDs, or attending clinics. In addition, a basic understanding of the horse's anatomy is important if I want to understand and relate to how I can ride my horse to promote long-term soundness. I must truly grasp the general needs that horses have. In every instance, I must educate myself, ask questions and observe how other good riders do it. Above all, I must learn to think independently and to always keep my mind awake and attentive.

I well remember the theoretical instruction my father gave me, my brother, and the other young riders at our riding association. We had to explain to him how to execute a half-halt or ride a certain movement.

*Jumping also develops the rider's feel for balance.*

Back then, my father also advised me, "Go to the arena and watch closely how the good riders work with their horses. You can learn a lot and observe many things." Often, he really did not say much when I rode. "If I'm not saying anything, it's a good sign," he told me. In this way, he wanted to guide me toward independence. I needed to determine for myself whether the horse was going well, so I concentrated fully on the horse and not on my dad. He only corrected me if something didn't seem right to him. After a successful test, he always praised me.

Afterward, we would go over the elements of the test or watch and analyze a video of the test together. We both took satisfaction from the strong and well-executed movements and then, back in training, I would focus my work on any weaknesses we observed. At the next test, I would then try to highlight these now improved elements.

My father was a thinker, and he really shared with me what it meant to have an alert mind. He made clear to me that although it's important to have an advisor and trainer, it is most important of all to think and feel independently when riding.

> "Before you can do it, you must understand it."
> Paul Stecken

*In order to give the correct aids, I need to first understand how and why I am riding an exercise.*

*My mare SAP Escada FRH has a strong character and is very refined and sensitive.*

## Building a Good Relationship

If I want to build unity with a horse, I need to listen really deeply and get on the same wavelength with him. A certain inner attitude is required to build a positive relationship. The power of positive thinking will carry over to the horse, and so will the power of negative thinking. I can only build a close relationship with my horse if I like him and I show him that.

Each horse has an entirely individual personality, just as we humans do. One personality type appeals to me more, another less. After some years, I know as a rider which types of horses I prefer, and which less so. I look for those that are a good fit for me. Still, it takes a while until I can really know the character of a horse. I'll have to live with some quirks and characteristics I may not prefer. However, I always try to have a positive influence on the horse's personality.

Through deliberate training, bad habits can become less pronounced but having said that, I must never allow myself to believe that I will be able to change the horse's essential character, which, I could not do if I wanted to — for example, a horse that tends toward "laziness" and would rather not try too hard.

# Empower Your Horse's Personality

To deliberately develop the horse's personality within his potential means to notice his personality, understand it, and cherish it: notice just how this creature is — with his strengths and his weaknesses. As such, I must not suppress his personality for any reason. This advice, too, was passed down to me from my dad. I need to completely take my cues from the horse, listen deeply, and remain very open to what comes forth.

With a shy horse, it can certainly take a while before he trusts you enough to show himself. In this case, I need to practice patience and not pressure him with too high expectations. I need to find out what gives him pleasure and which activities and tasks allow him to relax. By accomplishing this, I've already achieved a lot.

In contrast, with a confident horse, the challenge lies in maintaining and developing his significant motivation, while at the same time establishing a conscious basic obedience. My mare Escada is a good example. She is really ambitious with lots of courage and confidence, but at the same time has the tendency, especially in dressage, to be too independent from me. Since she already knows — for the most part — which element follows which in the test, she doesn't need me to provide the aids at all and would prefer to self-confidently anticipate every element of the test. It took a long time and many attempts at dressage tests until she finally learned to wait for my aids, and we continue to patiently work on this.

The balancing act lies in the fact that I want to cultivate autonomy in my horses and I don't want to suppress their willingness to perform, but at the same time, I cannot just be the "passenger." They must give me their complete attention, so that we are together in the same moment, concentrating on the same thing. With Escada, I got to that point by often taking her to dressage competitions so that she would get familiar with what is expected there. It also turned out to be good for her to have the experience of completing a dressage test and not automatically going cross-country the next day. This helped her relax more and develop an inner calm.

When riding a dressage test, I direct my thinking and aids very strongly onto the element we're doing in the moment. However, I also need to be ready to think about the correct execution of the next movement five to six seconds ahead of time. This means, the next movement is always already in my head. This can potentially cause a very refined, sensitive horse to anticipate. Should I punish a horse for thinking independently? No! I must, however, correct the horse consistently and with the necessary calmness, and have patience.

Horses also learn through regular repetition and persistent practice. It is important to always end with a good experience.

*Highest concentration in half-pass.*

*SAP Escada FRH learns to wait at the halt.*

## A Community Effort

As a team, we're unbeatable! I'm absolutely convinced of the truth of this sentence and I live it with enthusiasm. A true community equals happiness. When everyone knows his or her job and executes it with heart, enthusiasm, and determination, then this attitude and lifestyle becomes contagious. This inevitably leads to a positive environment, which can also help to support me on a not-so-good day.

Every barn needs a "good soul" who is there for the horses, looking

*We're a good team that can depend on one another and have lots of fun together.*

after them, keeping them in sight, feeling for them. This good soul will be the first to notice when a horse is not well or something is not right in the barn. For many years now, Carmen Thiemann has been my barn's good soul. No one knows my horses as well as she does. She has a natural gift for sensing how a horse feels in any given moment. Even those horses who tend to be shy and hold back open up to her. When a good spirit like this makes it her business to ensure a harmonious atmosphere in the barn, you can see the results in the horses. They appear happy and content.

*Carmen Thiemann is my barn manager — the "good soul" of the barn!*

With us, all horses are held in the same regard and receive the same level of care. Each of us pays diligent attention to the horses that are assigned to us. If we have the feeling that a horse needs some extra attention, he will get that special care. We make sure to only stable horses next to others that they like. This makes it much more likely they'll feel content in their stalls and be able to relax there. Even as we assign horses among our team members, we pay attention to which rider works especially well with each horse. This way, each horse has a specific person looking out for him. Sometimes we also make changes to these horse-and-rider matches; for example, when there is a phase where a horse and rider are no longer working together harmoniously.

## Think Like a Horse

For people like Carmen and me, who work with horses day in and day out, it gets easier to really listen deeply to the horses in our care, who we know inside-out. Many days, I am able to sense their actions and reactions a second sooner, and then promptly handle them in such a way so I prevent an error. The more established you are as a horse-and-rider team, and the more trust that exists there, the easier it will be to accomplish this.

With my horse Parmenides, who lives to jump and often bucks for joy after a fence, I can already sense at the takeoff whether or not he is going to buck on the landing. At this point, Parmi is 12 years old and we know each other well, as he came to me as a three-year-old. The bucking, which he's always loved to do, has never gone away. I can smile to myself about it and take pleasure in his motivation and enthusiasm for jumping.

*Parmenides just loves to jump.*

Especially with a young horse who may still be insecure in some situations, it is good for me as the rider to remain aware, putting myself in his position, which allows me to support him with very clear and definite aids. Optimally, I do this before the horse becomes insecure or makes a mistake. As the rider, I need to concentrate fully for this to succeed and to be be able to apply my aids as necessary.

## Learn from Mistakes

Of course, horses are going to make mistakes. For young horses, mistakes are an important part of learning. When I ask something, the horse seeks to answer. When he chooses the incorrect response, I correct the mistake very calmly and without getting aggravated. I then ride on, as if nothing happened.

As long as a young horse is not quite sure what the correct response is, he can only figure it out by trial and error. He'll learn best when I praise the correct response and ignore the incorrect one. This means I make a correction simply by carefully repeating the preparation for the task. When the rider praises him, the horse knows that was good. However, when a rider punishes him, the horse knows he's done something wrong, but he still doesn't know exactly what. Punishment and correction are two different things. Correction is an important part of guiding the horse to a correct response — above all, when he's learning a new exercise. In this case, I am consistent, clear, and also quite strict in asserting my correction. But, I'm never unfair and would prefer to go backward a step in the training before becoming so.

*Weisse Düne makes a very concentrated effort to respond correctly to the task at hand.*

*The young Trakehner stallion, Königssee, receives a versatile basic training and a consistent education.*

Horses want to complete their tasks well and respond correctly. When they do something well, such as mastering a new exercise like the flying change, and are praised for it, this increases their self-confidence and empowers their individual personality. If they are unfairly punished, they will eventually either pull back or become discontent. They won't develop a real trust for their rider and will remain insecure and skeptical, and in the worse cases, become unruly.

When jumping, horses also learn from their mistakes. For example, if a horse is not careful at a fence and causes a rail to fall, he will typically jump the next fence higher and more carefully. If a horse is clearly disobedient even though he is not being over-faced and he is familiar with the task, for example, by running out or refusing a small cross-rail, then I clearly and definitely apply my driving aids, reinforcing with crop or spurs, if necessary. I prevail, insisting on the completion of the task with increasingly strong aids. If necessary, I will reduce the difficulty and lower the fence, but the horse must go over it in every case. In order to avoid this kind of situation, it is advisable to put an experienced lead horse in place. The young, inexperienced horse trustfully follows his more experienced friend.

Also in dealing with stallions there are situations in which for safety reasons alone, I need to be strict — for example, unruly or aggressive behavior is never acceptable. A consistent basic training is absolutely vital for stallions, as an untrained stallion can put you in dangerous situations.

*The lead horse instills confidence.*

# Reinforce with Praise

If I want my horse to develop a confident and motivated personality, it's really important that I reinforce his good behavior with praise. With my encouragement, I can give the horse security, and this good feeling helps keep him happy. Praise can certainly look different depending on your horse's personality type. For example, I could praise my horse with a light tap or stroke on the neck or with a scratch to his withers. Some horses react really well to verbal praise from the rider. I've noticed that especially when riding the cross-country at events. I talk to my horses the whole time, praising them very clearly with words like "good," "super," and, "well done!" I really feel how much this renews their motivation.

During dressage tests, I sometimes use a discreet pat on the neck to praise my horse after he completes a successful exercise or one that he finds particularly difficult but has completed successfully. In every case, the horse takes this gesture to heart, noticing that I recognize and praise his efforts. The horse will also take to heart a cluck or a lightly spoken "good." These little things often mean a lot more than they appear to at first glance. Because horses are sensitive animals, I can also use a positive reinforcement like a word of praise to motivate them and keep them on my side.

When training at home, I like to incorporate a walk break as a reward. After a horse completes an especially difficult exercise or after a relatively long stretch of concentrated work, a horse can very clearly understand a break from work as a reward and will take it thankfully.

*The direction of the ear shows that my praise was noted.*

*"Well done, Alfi!"*

*A walk break is one form of praise, helping to relax body and mind.*

No matter how you reward your horse, it is important the reward comes at the right moment — namely, the moment when the horse has done something good. Continue to work calmly and consistently until your horse is willingly and obediently on your aids, trustfully accepting your lead. As soon as you've reached this moment, insert a walk break and praise him.

## Win Your Horse Over

It's ideal when we can start a young horse well from the beginning, training him with lots of time, calmness, and patience. He will then grow trustfully into his career as a riding horse, developing good self-confidence, and I can develop him in accordance with his innate talent.

To be honest, there will still be horses that, despite your best efforts, are still not really ready to exert themselves for their rider. These horses are missing the necessary willingness to perform, which I am dependent on as a rider if I want to progress with my horse.

My former dressage horse, Nector van het Carelshof, is a good example of how it is possible to win over a horse completely, even if you have not had the opportunity to start his training from the beginning yourself. It took me lots of time and patience to secure Nector's trust, but eventually we became a team and he fought for me.

At the age of 12, Nector arrived in my barn as a "finished" Grand Prix horse. But, in the beginning, he only wanted to run — he was much too hot to ride in a Grand Prix test. We spent the next six months riding out in the open, giving him lots of turnout and incorporating variety into his training, after which we competed in our first test at Second Level and did not place. Nector was still too nervous and insecure and, therefore, very uptight, tense, and tight.

Through Carmen's care and quiet work on basic training, incorporating many half-halts and First Level exercises, we reached the first step: supple relaxation. When finally the tension knots released and he came to fully trust Carmen and me, Nector gave us his whole heart, became very affectionate and enthusiastically showed us his strength in piaffe and passage. I never needed to drive him, only think about what I wanted him to do, and keep him calm. We achieved great placings and championships at the Grand Prix level, including seventh place in the 2002 World Cup Finals in Hertogenbosch and a win at Grand Prix and in the Freestyle in Stuttgart in 2002. Unfortunately, the two championships in Stuttgart were our last together — afterward, Nector was sold.

## Be Fair to the Horse

The perfect horse does not exist. In any case, I haven't met one yet. Every horse has strengths and weaknesses, which I get to know either very quickly or more slowly, depending on how intensively I can spend time with him. But one thing is certain: at some point, they become obvious, and therein lies the question of how I can best get along with him.

I take pleasure in my horse's strengths and praise him for them. Coping with his weaknesses is the real challenge. Over the years, I've learned there's no cookie-cutter solution. What helps with one horse may not necessarily work with another. I constantly need to adjust to the weaknesses of that particular horse, always seeking a solution. Some weaknesses, such as nervousness, lack of concentration, or insecurity, disappear as the horse gains more experience and the accompanying trust for his rider. Other weaknesses, however, can become more obvious as the horse's training advances. To this point, I'd like to share a few examples from my own horses. Maybe you have a similar horse at home in your barn and are having the same experiences that I am.

When we first began competing together, my mare Escada, for example, was very nervous and became explosive during dressage tests.

*In a dressage test, SAP Escada FRH is completely focused on the exercise.*

She could not focus on me very well at all. This behavior improved with time, thanks to a more established routine and experience for her, and to increased inner calm and concentration for me. Still, I must always remain aware and continue to work steadily on her internal relaxation. I believe Escada will find calmness and relaxation, which are necessary for a completely harmonious dressage performance. She's shown me more than once that she is capable of this: for example, in 2015 when we won the Four Star event in Luhmühlen and the Three Star in Aachen. On those occasions, we were able to put forth expressive and harmonious dressage tests.

With my dressage horse, Dresden Mann, who is a stallion, there was always the problem that he got distracted very quickly by his environment. Some days, I did not have a chance at keeping him interested in me. As soon as other horses appeared, he could only be ridden with great difficulty. I had to realize that his stallion behaviors stood in the way of his potential as a Grand Prix dressage horse. Even with consistent training and lots of groundwork, we only managed to make ourselves attractive to him some of the time. The hormones were simply stronger.

As a stallion, Alfi could never get calm when other horses were near him. As this became clear to us, we decided, together with his owner, that he should be gelded. Today, I can say for sure that gelding Alfi was the best decision. As a gelding, he is a very sociable and people-oriented horse. He remains a dominant horse, but during a test, he now always gives me his full and total concentration and he wants to get everything right. He did retain one stallion-like quality: Alfi is still a little show-off. When we enter the arena at competitions, he always grows at least half an inch. He really couldn't do anything about his earlier weakness — he was simply being controlled by hormones.

My longtime championship horse Abraxxas is a very special one. With him, I have experienced emotional highs and lows, unlike any horse before him. In dressage, Braxxi gave me some unbelievably beautiful moments. These were glimpses at pure harmony, which I will never forget. Cross-country, we were a well-matched team. He always fought like a lion, trusting me to find the best way for us, and he was as fast as a "little horse" his size could be. He simply gave it all for me. Often, after the dressage and cross-country phases, we would be in the lead heading into the final phase, show-jumping. And there came the letdown. Show-jumping was Braxxi's worst discipline. He simply wasn't careful and made jumping errors. It was always a high and low, and I admit, I was often very disappointed after the show-jumping phase.

The height of my disappointment was the 2011 European Eventing Championships in Luhmühlen. Here, we were once again in the lead before show-jumping, but Braxxi made six jumping errors, so in the end, we only finished tenth. As I rode out of that show-jumping arena,

*Alfi likes to make himself "big."*

*Abraxxas on the show-jumping course at the World Games in Kentucky, ridden in a hackamore.*

I would have liked to head directly to the highway and gallop all the way back to my barn in Munster! A day later, I'd begun to wrap my head around it, but this rollercoaster of feelings, going from victory to defeat, still made it difficult for me to get ahold of my normally very steady nerves.

Of course, I tried for years to find a solution. We tried out many variations of training techniques, equipment, and work. But in the end, with Braxxi, it always came down to the day. It didn't matter whether the course was set very high or super easy: a clean round was an exception for him. Was this just laziness? Did he simply know that it didn't matter if he touched those poles, in contrast to the fixed obstacles when going cross-country? Even now, I really can't say for sure. I only know that I spent a whole lot of time thinking about it and never reached a solution.

The final sentence on this topic was spoken by a friend of mine, "There are some things you can't change. You just have to accept them, so that you can better live with them." Thanks to this very true and wise advice I came to terms with Abraxxas's big personality. I am grateful to him for so many of the most wonderful and exceptional moments of my riding life. Twice, we won Team Gold medals at the

*I'm delighted after the dressage phase.*

Olympic Games and we were European Team Champions. Without him, I may not have had all of these experiences.

In the later years, I got better and better at living with his weaknesses. I adjusted my expectations to match reality and no longer hoped to win individual medals. When it did happen, I was even more thrilled, but at some point it was no longer important to me. For the team competition, I was always a strong cornerstone. I could enjoy the ride with Braxxi so much more fully. At our last Four Star event together in Burghley, I experienced every moment with such awareness. It was our most difficult cross-country course and I felt a huge responsibility to guide us to the finish, safe and sound. But Braxxi outdid himself and we finished in fourth place.

With great respect and deep appreciation, I take a bow to this horse who always gave his all, but simply did not jump so well over colorful poles.

## See the Good and Develop It

By nature, I am a positive person. I take great pleasure over small things throughout the day and quickly move past small annoyances. That's my attitude toward life, guiding me through. If I want to change or achieve something, I keep the goal in sight. Even with young horses whose potential and characteristics are not yet 100 percent recognizable, I paint a mental picture of where the future may take them. A rider needs imagination and I consciously direct mine toward developing the positive potential in each horse.

## Why I Ride in Dressage, Show-Jumping, and Eventing

All three disciplines have a big attraction for me. I was very fortunate to have had a classical riding education growing up. From almost as soon as I could walk, my father was passing on to me how to truly educate a horse. He showed me how dressage can be elevated to art, when a rider employs the aids "with feel" for the horse, training him to go from his own accord as much as possible. My father made sure that he was empowering the horse's personality so that the horse would shine in the arena and approach the whole thing with lots of confidence.

For me, dressage means the highest level of concentration and perfection. Good dressage riding is art in full harmony as the horse responds to my imperceptible aids, though the spectator cannot see them. Above all, when riding a freestyle, I can emphasize the artistic elements and allow my horse to shine. My father often said, "The horse

*Horseware Hale Bob OLD — brave and fast.*

*Franziskus and I enjoy schooling dressage in an open field.*

must dance, emerging from himself. We want to see his personality, not just an expressionless run-through of the exercise."

He also always encouraged me to ride a dressage exercise boldly forward and to take risks in my riding. For example, I always prefer to go all out when riding the extended canter. "He's not going to take off with you," I hear my father saying. He's right, I think, always with a smile.

In eventing, on the other hand, the challenge is to ride all the different disciplines with one horse. The horse must really trust his rider in order to successfully complete the challenging cross-country course. The happiness is, therefore, so much greater when you conquer a cross-country course together as a team. It's a very special experience when you're with your horse 10 minutes into cross-country and you still have difficult questions to answer on course, galloping from jump to jump, the harmony between horse and rider remaining true, with the horse giving everything to you over and over again. In this way,

*All my horses regularly do hill work. This strengthens the muscles, increases condition, and helps to balance the mind.*

something comes together and it results in a deep, trusting bond between human and horse.

The forward gallop on a cross-country course captures the horse's natural drive to movement. Jumping over the cross-country obstacles requires his courage, dexterity, and level-headedness. The dressage test at a three-day event requires the horse to be obedient, "through" with willing cooperation, relaxed, and supple. The show-jumping component is similar. Here, I need the highest level of concentration and precision, good coordination and a feel for rhythm. If I want to remain error-free on the show-jumping course, my horse needs to be finely tuned to my aids. In jumping, the quality of the horse plays a deciding role: the horse must have the right capacity, carefulness, and attitude to avoid knocking down rails. The more perfectly the rider can support her horse, the greater the likelihood of a clean round — and often, a little luck also comes into play.

## Variety in Dressage Training

As all my horses are trained for versatility, those that later specialize as dressage horses continue to enjoy rich variety in their training. They gather valuable experience outside the dressage arena. We practice dressage exercises while out hacking on hills or in an open field. Riding hills increases condition and strengthens musculature, especially in the hindquarters and back. The horses are being challenged, but they don't notice the effort so much, because at the same time they are taking in the environment, the changes in footing, and the horses in front or behind them. These diverse impressions and experiences contribute to my horse's calmness and balance. All my horses are ridden regularly over cavalletti, longed, and jumped over small fences.

The cavalletti work not only brings diversity to the daily training, it strengthens the horse and allows me to reach and develop specific muscle groups really effectively. At the same time, the horses are learning to work in partnership with the rider of their own accord and to react quickly. In fact, with cavalletti work or gymnastic jumping, horses must sometimes make a decision independently, seeking a solution. These qualities, such as critical thinking or self-confidence, are those I actively want to develop in my dressage horses. I also notice that this type of training does these horses good, improving their balance, clear-headedness, and increasing motivation.

## Key Points for Eventing Horses

In its focus on riding cross-country, the training of the event horses naturally distinguishes itself clearly from the training of the dressage horse. By practicing the discipline of dressage, these "field horses" can certainly learn a thing or two from the dressage horses. These include qualities such as obedience, discipline, and patience. A dressage test puts great weight on correctness and precision. The horse needs to listen to the rider, reacting to refined aids. In the dressage arena, the event horse must, above all, learn to scale back his independence a bit and allow himself to be guided by the rider. This is difficult for many event horses because when going cross-country, their independent attitude and critical thinking are exactly what is needed.

I feel that it is often good for an event horse when I start him off by going to dressage competitions in order to school the qualities that are required in that discipline. I've noticed I am much more successful at producing obedience, calmness, and the necessary patience in the horse when I incorporate a dressage-only competition or two during the winter or at the beginning of a season. This goes for show-jumping, too. For example, going to several show-jumping competitions has done my event horse Hale Bob a world of good in terms of schooling his rideability on the show-jumping course.

*The expressive SAP Escada FRH strikes off really well from behind in Caen at the World Equestrian Games, 2014.*

## The Weekly Training Program

Although our training is based on the needs of each individual horse, I do have some definite rules related to how a training plan is formed. Every horse gets at least one day off each week. This means he is not ridden or worked with in any other way, but instead is turned out for most of the day. One day of each week, every horse is longed in sliding side-reins, working over cavalletti. At my place, cavalletti are set up in the arena at all times, so that I can also build in work with them at any point during a ride.

Once a week, we incorporate jumping — which goes for the dressage horses, too. A weekly ride out in the open is very important to me,

*Once a week, jumping is part of every horse's training plan.*

which at our place could mean either riding in an open pasture or doing hill work. This not only improves conditioning, but does both horse and rider good. On the other three to four days of the week, dressage riding is our focus. Sometimes with young horses, it makes the most sense to practice new exercises on back-to-back days in order to solidify the lesson.

Most of the time, my plan for dressage work is as follows: one day of reviewing the basics. This means I don't introduce any new exercises that day, but rather reinforce what the horse already knows and focus on "throughness" with willing cooperation. The horse should remain relaxed and honest as he responds to very refined aids, and half-halts are paramount. I always begin with an extended warm-up phase and ride lots of transitions.

One day a week, I ride a dressage test. This way the horse learns to expect to be ridden through many elements in succession, and still execute them properly. It is important to practice this regularly at home, as only then can I confidently call upon my horse to perform these exercises consecutively at a competition.

It's always an interesting task to teach a new exercise to a young horse. For this, I need to really take my time and think carefully about this individual horse and how to move forward with him. I learn very quickly which exercises are easy for a horse and which ones are problematic. For example, Franziskus seemed to learn flying changes all by himself, whereas in the beginning, Geraldine found these extraordinarily difficult. With canter pirouettes, it was then the exact opposite. This shows once again that there is no cookie-cutter approach. I need to adjust to every horse and find how he learns best. Sometimes, it can take longer than one off-season for the horse to learn the elements needed to progress to the next level.

Figuring out just how much I can demand is sometimes a real balancing act. Naturally, it can be physically difficult for a horse to learn new exercises. And, once in a while, I need to push my horse's physical limits and increase the intensity of the training if I want to be effective. But it's most important that my horse stays in good spirits through this. He must want to try for me; otherwise, I do not have any chance of increasing my horse's performance.

But how do I get a horse to want to try for me?

First of all, I need to make the exercise appeal to him so he hardly notices the increased effort. Through praise and recognition, I set the tone with encouragement, and I motivate the horse to keep trying. And, before it gets too difficult, or he loses his energy and begins making mistakes, I need to stop or take a break. It's not always easy to choose the right moment for this. If I always stop too soon, my horse won't continue to develop. But, if I stop too late even just once, I risk developing discontent. When I treat my horse as a partner and support him as best I can, then as a rule it works out okay for me when I push his limits and really ask him to try hard. It's only with this belief as my starting point that I can develop a horse to the highest levels.

Performance capacity can weaken quickly, especially with young horses. Here, I really need to listen deeply to my horse and figure out why he cannot bring his best performance on any given day. Does he not feel good physically because he's going through a growth spurt? Is he overwhelmed by this exercise, or is he simply lacking motivation today? The better I know my equine partner, the better chance I have of finding the right answer.

At all times, I need to keep in mind that my horse is stronger than I am. I can never win by force. For this reason, among other things, I

*Geraldine looks relaxed and*
*attentive for dressage work.*

*Franziskus — dressage champion through Prix St. George.*

*Parmenides — champion Advanced Level show jumper.*

lean strongly away from the use of draw reins. When I engage even once in a battle of force with the horse, it creates the potential for the horse to get a sense of his physical superiority. Obviously, I believe in a basic level of obedience and I work through any given task with patience, persistence, and necessary consequences. I feel that consistent, responsible behavior toward the horse is the most important inner quality that I must have as a rider, and indeed as a person. Our team's entire operation is based on working with one another in a helpful and attentive way. The horses and humans on our team all work hard and purposefully, and we have a responsibility toward one another.

## Enjoy Your Work and Ensure Variety

As part of these caring relationships, we consciously take time to enjoy activities and have adventures together. For example, in addition to riding together out in the open on a regular basis, we take the horses swimming in the summertime and even take them with us to the North Sea on vacation. Relaxing together, experiencing nature together and enjoying a wide variety of places is just as restful for the people as for the horses.

*Riding with a neck ring is a pleasure.*

Even in the day-to-day, we make sure to incorporate the necessary variety. Riding bareback and with just a neck ring is part of this. As soon as we ride the horses in the neck ring alone, they immediately have a different facial expression. Since we can't depend on any equipment, we must pay more attention to one another than usual and be very refined with our aids. This schools sensitivity in both horse and rider. This always serves me well when I'm later in situations requiring quick reactions. Only then will I truly know how refined my communication with my horse is. In addition, it's simply a great pleasure to ride your horse in only a neck ring and that's another reason that I do it regularly. Certainly, it needs to be incorporated in small steps and practiced.

Riding bareback is fun for me and awakens lots of childhood memories. Back then, I'd often play around bareback with my pony. Today, I believe that this is one of the ways a rider can learn to better follow her horse's movement. Likewise, groundwork is another activity we enjoy. I especially like the playful aspects, and the fact that these exercises bring you closer to the horse. Groundwork also has an educational element that I find especially valuable when working with young horses and stallions. We use groundwork exercises to relax the horse and for obedience training.

## A Horse-Centered Approach

To me, it seems obvious that performance horses should be kept in the way that is most appropriate to their species. This means, they get to move freely every day, whether in a paddock or out at pasture. They need social contact or their herd, in order for them to feel safe and well. My horses are turned out daily in the fresh air — no matter the season. If they are clipped and it is raining or cold outside, they wear a blanket for protection. In summer, they wear fly sheets.

*Horseware Hale Bob OLD enjoys his free time.*

*Rolling is part of his wellness program.*

*Performance horses can also be turned out to pasture in groups, as long as they get along.*

In my experience, horses that are turned out regularly rarely hurt themselves. The danger is much greater with horses only turned out sporadically that then naturally need to explode. I can never be 100 percent sure a horse won't injure himself — that's totally clear, but I'm aware of this and live with it. Should an emergency occur, I have to accept the loss. Horses hurt themselves just as often in stalls, on trailers, and when ridden. Over the years, we will see injuries that were totally unpredictable and unavoidable. To me, it's more important that my horses get to live in accordance with their needs as much as they possibly can. I feel responsible for making this happen. If I couldn't turn them out freely, I would not want to keep horses anymore.

Even at competitions, they do not have to go without turnout. We set up small temporary paddocks for them so that they can graze and roll. We're happy to sit nearby and watch them closely.

We almost always train our horses in groups. There is, of course, a practical reason for this, as we need to use the indoor arena or riding ring simultaneously in order to get all the horses worked. For cavalletti work, jumping, going cross-country or riding hills, the more experienced horses are often utilized as a lead horse. Young horses must, at first, get used to the fact that other horses will be coming toward them and worked around them. Later, training together provides security, which allows them to work in a relaxed atmosphere. Of course, they must learn to be ridden alone. We'll practice that, for example, by riding a dressage test alone in the indoor arena. By and by, it becomes routine.

# The Right Equipment

Suitable equipment is important to every responsible and aware rider. Naturally, saddle and bridle must fit correctly so the horse will feel good and stay sound. This is as much a given as attentive care, good feed, a horse-centered attitude, and appropriate work.

### SADDLE

I don't intend to go into great detail about specific equipment, but rather to speak a bit about the general topic of tack and equipment, according to the Klimke tradition. In my opinion, a piece of equipment is not necessarily good, just because it is modern. For example, I'm not an advocate of dressage saddles furnished with thick knee rolls that jam the rider into position. I prefer a flatter saddle with less knee roll so I can sit closer to the horse and follow his movement well.

For cross-country, a flat seat is important, so that I have enough freedom of movement when jumping banks. Here, not-too-thick knee rolls are helpful for supporting the position of the thigh. Going cross-country, the leg position must always remain secure, even as the upper body tilts back at a bank jump.

*Cross-country saddle with a flat seat.*

### GIRTH

At my place, you will still see the old cord girths used with dressage saddles. This is for the simple reason that with these girths, the saddles sit well and the pressure is distributed evenly when the girth is tightened. I don't have to make the girth too tight and can thereby avoid pressure in the girth area. In addition, they come up higher, which is good because I really prefer to tighten the girth once I'm on the horse, especially with nervous or very sensitive horses. With these girths, I don't have to bend so far over in order to tighten. That's much easier and more comfortable, especially with young horses.

### BREASTPLATE/MARTINGALE/NECK STRAP

In show-jumping or jumping cross-country, even a well-fitting saddle can slip backward. A breastplate helps to maintain the saddle's optimal position. As a rider, I can also grab the breastplate with one hand in an emergency, in order to hold on. In addition, the martingale is attached to the breastplate. A neck strap, which I like to use when riding out in the open, can also be used to hold onto and helps to support the aids for downward transitions.

When riding cross-country, I don't use a martingale because the horse uses his neck as a balancing rod. A too short martingale can especially limit the horse's freedom of movement when jumping down from a bank or into a water obstacle.

In my entire life, I have never used draw reins and will not do so in

*A dressage saddle with sparse knee rolls and a cord girth.*

the future. My horses are not forced into a frame, but rather develop their position over many years of training.

## BITS

In my wishful thinking, I always want to ride in a loose-ring snaffle, in all three disciplines. However, for going cross-country, it can be advantageous to have a strong bit, such as an elevator or a gag bit, to be able to reduce the tempo quickly at a crucial moment. This is also important for safety reasons. It must always be possible for me to slow my horse down in order to prepare him as I approach a jump.

## CAVESSONS

For "normal" day-to-day training, an English cavesson is my standard equipment. I like to change it up from time to time and ride in a drop noseband, instead. I do so because with the drop noseband, the

*English cavesson with flash noseband.*

pressure is not only on the bars of the mouth and the poll, but rather is also distributed over the nose, which allows me to influence the horse more effectively and lightly. Having said that, a drop noseband does not work on every horse. Some horses don't find it comfortable. With a figure-eight noseband, which I often use for riding cross-country, the straps cross higher up on the nose. Therefore, the horse has a lot of freedom to breathe.

### SPURS

I ride all my horses using short, dull spurs, both for schooling work and ideally also in competition. Normally, the inside of my calf lies relaxed against the horse's side, so the spurs don't come into use. If my horse does not respond to my driving leg aids, then I can give one short driving aid with the spurs, which reminds the horse he should react immediately to the aid from my calf the next time. If he reacts appropriately, I praise him and I know that the next time I will only need to use the inside of my leg for the aid. Chris Bartle says, "Every horse is sensitive enough to feel a fly land on him." This means the horse knows exactly when and where the leg aid is being given and the driving leg is being used. "So, train him to respond when you whisper with your aids."

### WHIPS

I seldom ride with a whip and use it very specifically because I don't want to become dependent on using one. However, if I need the whip for a reason it's there — in which case, I use it quickly and then hold it passively again so that neither my horse nor I myself get used to it.

In three-day eventing, competitors are not allowed to carry a whip for dressage, which is the same rule as for international dressage. We want to condition the horse to be ridden from refined aids, so from the beginning, he should become accustomed to this. It's an important goal to give aids that are as invisible as possible.

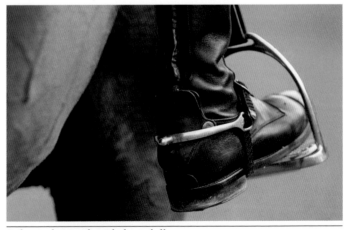

*I almost always ride with short, dull spurs.*

*At "Open Training" I am happy to answer questions about horse training.*

## Exemplify Openness

Like everyone else, I put my pants on one leg at a time, cannot work miracles, and encounter situations where I have no idea what to do. I don't have any secrets and I want to share my work with horses clearly and in a way that is accessible to all. This openness is one of my life principles. Once a month, I host an "Open Training," which can be audited by anyone who is interested in seeing how I train my horses and apprentices. It brings me great pleasure to share my knowledge and pass it along. In my opinion, we can all learn through this kind of open exchange of information, allowing us to develop further. Horses also learn through these open trainings. For example, even the young horses are already learning to cope with crowds along the rail.

# The People

*...who support me, stand by my side, inspire me and
play a big role in my life.*

## My Family

My parents always supported my riding. Much of what I know about
horses, I learned from my father. He imparted enthusiasm and love for
horses, and instilled in me a fascination with equestrian sports. He was
my rock.

How often we spoke about the training of horses. I remember his
words so well and as I make my own way, I always feel grateful for the
advice he impressed upon me.

In difficult situations, before big decisions, or when I face questions to which I have no answers, I take the time to think about and
consider what my father would have done.

My mother has always taken great pleasure in helping me. During
the Olympic Games in Athens and Hong Kong, she looked after my
daughter, Greta. We meet up as often as possible and then always
engage in intense discussion about the hustle and bustle of our daily
lives.

My brother, Rolf, is a trusted companion. He enthusiastically

*Daughter Philippa and Nemo also trot up hills.*

*Andreas is always happy to accompany me.*

*Andreas, Greta, Philippa, and I enjoy spending time together with the horses.*

attends every important event. I can always rely on him and he is always there for me when I need him.

My brother Michael is an advisor in all aspects of life. When I select horses, his opinion is important and his instruction and help at dressage competitions means a lot to me. We're always there for one another and we're connected by more than just riding. When we get his two sons and my two daughters together, we always have lots of fun.

My husband, Andreas, stands by me no matter what and provides great advice. He sees the big picture and stays calm and relaxed in every situation. Andreas is a great dad and accompanies me and our daughters to competitions. He shares my enthusiasm for horses and when he's riding, he's smiling!

My family is my anchor. Whether we're laughing, chatting, or having fun adventures with the kids, they have my heart. It's a wonderful balance for what can be a very tightly scheduled workload.

Carmen Thiemann, my barn manager, is also part of the family. She began her apprenticeship in my father's barn at the age of 17. In 1998, we established our own training and competition barn. Carmen and I trust one another deeply. We know one another inside out and understand each other perfectly. Carmen makes people and horses happy, is tireless in her efforts, and always puts her heart and soul into it. As the years go by, she has taken on more and more responsibility, so

*Carmen Thiemann.*

that she now manages the barn with complete independence and I am free to really concentrate on riding. Carmen is irreplaceable — also as Greta's godmother!

My team and my close friends, who are too numerous for me to name here, share my life with all its highs and lows. Beneficial conversation, regular outings for the good of the soul, emotional connection, fun and joy, as well as sharing relaxing times together — I don't want to miss any of this and I take as much time for it as possible.

## Paul Stecken

After the death of my father in 1999, Mr. Stecken called me out of the blue to offer his help and support in the training of my horses. I gratefully accepted his offer and am happy to have a person with such immense experience on my side.

He supports me in training my horses in dressage and instructs my apprentices in riding theory. His theoretical and practical knowledge along with his wealth of experience are immeasurable. He possesses an outstanding ability to explain concepts. When it comes to assessing horses, his opinion is of great importance to me. The "hippology discussions" we engage in are sometimes like a trip to another time period. After my father's death, Mr. Stecken and I spent many long evenings revising the first edition of Basic Training of the Young Horse, updating the text and choosing new photos.

*Paul Stecken.*

*Hans Melzer.*

*Christopher Bartle.*

# Hans Melzer and Christopher Bartle

Since 2000, Hans Melzer and Christopher Bartle have been the national trainers for the German eventing team. The two of them support us riders as only they can do. Hans and Chris are very important advisors. They have a good eye for which horse and rider will work well together. Way back when, they discovered and procured Braxxi for me. I also have Hans to thank for Weisse Düne. When I try out a new horse, I always ask Hans and Chris for their opinion. Hans is an unshakeable optimist, always looking ahead, and motivates me tremendously, along with the rest of the eventing team. Both work to ensure very open and honest communication. They have good antennae for how we riders are feeling and they always see to it that we're doing well. Hans has a talent for organizing and communicating. He is a man of action and, if necessary, he will drag the dressage arena or fill holes on the cross-country course himself.

Training with Hans and Chris, walking the cross-country course with them at competitions and analyzing it together, is very important. Both of them always spend lots of time on this, so that I am completely prepared to ride the cross-country phase. I credit Chris Bartle with teaching me the meaning of safe riding when going cross-country, with complete thoroughness and clarity. Over time, I have internalized his rules with the goal being that I can call them up at all times. Thanks to Chris, I learned the basics of the all-important defensive seat necessary for cross-country and I always continue to work on this. With Chris, I developed a conditioning system using hill work and established a definite training plan. We analyze videos from competitions and consider in which places there is the possibility for improvement. When I plan a competitive season, I speak with both trainers together and we plan the targeted entries for each horse on an individual basis.

It's simply a pleasure to work with Hans and Chris and they both deserve much credit for our success in these past years.

## Kurt Gravemeier

I can always count on Kurt. He was my jumping trainer even back before the 2000 Olympic Games. When he travels along to an important competition or championship, I always feel especially secure. Together, we inspect the show-jumping course and he helps me with my warm-up over fences. For many years now, I have trained with him regularly with different horses on various show-jumping courses, so that the horses and I get in the routine and are continually developing ourselves. Thanks to Kurt, I won my first Advanced Level show-jumping competition.

Kurt gives constructive criticism, remains open to new ideas, and always speaks freely. He calls a spade a spade, even when I have ridden poorly on occasion. Kurt loyally stuck by me, even as Braxxi's weakness for show-jumping became clearer and clearer. During that time, he sent me to Marcus Ehning to try to problem-solve before the World Equestrian Games in Kentucky. I'm grateful that he always finds time for me and that I can train with him. In selecting and assessing new horses, Kurt's opinion is very important. Today, I would never buy an event horse without having first jumped the horse with Kurt. We plan competitions and consult often about the development and career path of a horse, in order to decide the way forward together. Over many years, we've become a well-coordinated team and he knows me only too well.

*Kurt Gravemeier.*

## Wilfried Gehrmann

Wilfried Gehrmann comes to my place once a week to do in-hand work with my horses. He works with the horses on either a double-longe or in long-lines. This is how we initially approach piaffe and passage when developing young horses. Through this work, the horses increase their power and we develop their readiness for collection. Wilfried works with the young horses from the ground, with a helper walking next to the horse in the beginning. Working from the ground, his aids are given with exacting precision, touching a horse's leg at exactly the right moment so that the horse understands very quickly which leg he should be moving when.

In this way, the horse learns his first half-steps very quickly. It's very important to take a break after just a few successful steps and offer praise. This way, tension does not build in the horse and the trust remains. You can never underestimate how much power the horse must use to collect for piaffe and passage. Less is more with this! All horses are very grateful for regular pauses for treats.

*Wilfried Gehrmann supports me with in-hand work.*

With the horses that are further along in their training, we work together on piaffe and passage. This means, I give the aids from the saddle, and Wilfried supports me from the ground. With this set-up, the horses are eager and motivated. Here, too, it is always wonderful to see the effect of encouraging praise. Thanks to his extensive experience, Wilfried Gehrmann remains completely quiet, calm, and clear as he supports the horses and guides them along.

## Peter Kreinberg

My first interaction with the well-known trainer and Western rider, Peter Kreinberg, took place many years ago at the equestrian festival, Equitana. We rode in a demonstration that involved us switching horses and I noticed that his horse was completely calm, relaxed, and well-trained, but still very awake and present. The more he told me about his training method, The Gentle Touch, the clearer it became to me that he must visit our training barn. I wanted to learn more about his philosophy and was especially interested in his assessment of difficult stallions.

From Peter Kreinberg, Carmen and I learned a lot about the behavior and personality of our horses: I like to ask him for advice because he can assess the horse's personality so accurately. With Franziskus, Peter Kreinberg very quickly unmasked the sensitivity that was hiding beneath his macho affect. In essence, Franz is a really sweet guy who will, I hope, continue to develop well with clear leadership.

It's always exciting to change things up with Peter and Rika Kreinberg — it's a good way to see beyond the limits of my own riding style.

*Peter Kreinberg.*

# Veterinarian Dr. Ina Gösmeier

I've been friends with Dr. Ina Gösmeier for a long time now. She travels with the German riders to the important competitions and championships and is responsible for the integrated health care provided to the horses. Above and beyond this role, she is, for me, a valuable supporter. As a veterinarian, she incorporates traditional Chinese medicine into her practice, treating horses with acupuncture and Chinese herbs. She visits my barn regularly and treats my horses with acupuncture, helping to support their overall health. In addition, by classifying the horses into the "types" of traditional Chinese medicine, I learn a lot about their character, constitution, and learning style. For example, I was able to both understand and respond much better to Geraldine's cautious behavior after learning from Dr. Gösmeier that Geraldine is a shen, or kidney, type.

Every horse has individual physical and mental idiosyncrasies, which can be positively influenced by acupuncture. Through Ina, I had my first experiences with natural horsemanship and groundwork. While Alfi was still a stallion, I often sought her advice. I deeply value Ina's opinion and medical competence. When I have a new horse at the barn to try out, her professional assessment is always a deciding factor as she really helps me to evaluate the horse from a different point of view. Her approach is always holistic, meaning she gives equal weight to physical and mental characteristics. She's a highly perceptive person, which not only the horses sense and value.

*Veterinarian Dr. Ina Gösmeier.*

# Linda Tellington-Jones

Linda Tellington-Jones, founder of the Tellington Method and TTOUCH, uses soft touches to build horses' trust, allowing them to feel better physically, learn more efficiently, and be able to relax. I got to know Linda in 1989 when she visited my father and our family and introduced us to her method.

In 2008, I had the opportunity to invite Linda to my training barn to work with me and my horses. She showed me different TTouches and further examples of her Tellington techniques for bodywork and groundwork.

She observed closely as I practiced dressage. When I rode a pirouette on my horse Damon Hill, Linda called out, "Dance with him!" The mental picture of dancing together helped me ride a good and rhythmic pirouette.

From Linda, I also came to know and value riding with a neck ring. The Ear and Mouth TTouches help my horses to relax after they travel. I highly value Linda as an admirable person, who has done so much good for horses.

*Linda Tellington-Jones.*

## My Horse Owners

Without the incredible support of my horses' owners, I would not be able to compete. I am so grateful for the trusting and long-lasting partnerships I enjoy with all of them. Their commitment is the basis for my successful riding. It is always a pleasure when an owner attends the training or competition with us, and directly experiences the horse's development. We have a shared responsibility to the horses and experience the highs and lows together. I value the open, mutual discussion and the deep trust they extend daily to me and my team.

I owe my thanks to so many owners who have supported me over a long time — so many that I unfortunately lack the space to name them all. To represent my gratitude to all of them, I would like to thank Madeleine Winter-Schulze here. After the 2008 Olympic Games in Hong Kong, Braxxi's then owner wished to sell him. For a long time, we lived in fear that he would be purchased by another rider. Madeleine was the first to offer to help by purchasing Braxxi. It is only thanks to her generous support that I was able to continue riding him. Still today, Braxxi remains a part of the family.

Then, when we sought an owner to purchase Escada, Madeleine again stepped forward. She gives me complete freedom with these horses and thanks to her, I have the feeling that Braxxi and Escada are my own horses. Madeleine likes to attend the big championships and takes great pleasure, as we all do, in Escadas's considerable success.

*Madeleine Winter-Schulze.*

In the Chapter "My Horses," you can find more detail about my horses' owners.

## My Partners and Sponsors

In order to have long-lasting success in competitive riding, I rely on the support of my partners and sponsors, with whom I enjoy a good, and for the most part, long-term connection. To them, I owe the fact that my horses and I are always perfectly turned out and have the best equipment we could ask for in our work. I also so enjoy working with my sponsors and partners on the development and use of new products, where I can weigh in by applying my practical experience and knowledge. In this way, their support constitutes the basis of our work and our joint success. Therefore, I'd especially like to take the opportunity here to deeply thank all of my patrons, sponsors, and partners for our trusting and loyal collaboration. Without you, it simply would not be possible to pursue my dream job — competitive riding — in this form. So, I hope for a continued good and long collaboration as well as continued joint success. It applies here, too: as a team, we're unbeatable!

Further information about my partners and sponsors can be found on page 170.

# The Olympics
## — A Family Tradition

*I grew up with the Olympic Games. From 1964 on, my father regularly took part in the Games. He won six gold and two bronze medals. Up until the 2000 Summer Olympic Games, he had remained the most successful German Olympian for many years.*

The Olympics were always a big element of our lives. We knew an Olympic year would be a special year with many exciting experiences. My father considered his horses in terms of a four-year rhythm based on the timing of the Olympic Games. He always said, "The end of the Games is the beginning of the Games." Meaning, he thought carefully about which one of his horses would be able to take part in the next Olympics based on which horse was the right age and at a suitable level of training.

One of his biggest successes at the Olympic Games took place at the 1984 Games in Los Angeles, when he rode Ahlerich to win the individual gold medal in dressage. However, for me, the many Team Gold medals were also unforgettable. My father was always so proud to have the opportunity to represent his country. At his last Olympic Games in 1988 in Seoul, he was Germany's flag bearer during the opening ceremony. I looked on proudly from the stands. In Seoul, he won his last gold medal.

A great wish of my father's was for one of his children to follow in his footsteps and one day participate in the Olympic Games. Therefore, when I first participated in the Olympics, in Sydney in 2000, it was very emotional. My father had passed away the year before — way too soon. I thought about how wonderful it would have been for him to be there as I rode in my first Olympic Games. My entire family was in Sydney and the time we spent there together was really intense. We took pleasure in the outstanding performance of my horse, Sleep Late, as he completed the demanding cross-country course both error-free

01

02

03

01 *My first Olympic Games in Sydney with Sleep Late.*

02 *Dr. Reiner Klimke and Ahlerich at the 1984 Olympic Games in Los Angeles.*

03 *Taking great pleasure in gold at the 2008 Olympic Games in Hong Kong.*

and without time penalties. I knew deep down that my father was there with me, looking over our performance and helping to keep us safe. As a team, we finished fourth in Sydney and I was very pleased with my horse's performance.

In 2004, I again rode Sleep Late in the Olympic Games, which this time took place in Athens. Again, the Games had a special emotional meaning for me, as the cross-country phase took place on the anniversary of my father's death. My brothers flew in for the day and we kept one another very close. As a team we won the event, with Bettina Hoy taking the individual gold; however, we later had to give these medals back, as Bettina had ridden twice over the start line in the show-jumping phase. It was a real crime and in the end we were all so disappointed. But, afterward, everyone knew of us and in the hearts of our supporters, we were the Olympic champions.

01

02

01 *At the 2012 London Olympic Games: Riding cross-country on FRH Butts Abraxxas.*

02 *On the podium: My second team Olympic gold medal at the 2012 Olympic Games.*

03 *The height of concentration and harmony in the dressage test.*

Four years later, at the 2008 Games in Hong Kong, our time had come. We wanted to show that we really were the best. We took gold as a team and Hinrich Romeike won the individual gold. It was an incomparable joy; our team spirit was enormous and we heartily celebrated our gold medal win.

The 2012 Olympic Games in London were my fourth — there, I won my second Team Gold medal riding Abraxxas. For me, it was one of the best rides ever on Braxxi and a highpoint of our joint career. A harmonious dressage test, a fantastic cross-country ride, and a good, for him, show-jumping round. I was touched by his fighting spirit and his trust in me. I consciously savored every moment.

03

When I stand on the podium, hear the German national anthem, and hold a medal in my hand, I always look upward — to my dad. I feel such a deep connection to him.

I was able to keep the Klimke family tradition going at the 2016 Olympic Games in Rio, where I won a team silver medal on Bobby. For me, it is still the case that an Olympic year is special. There's a certain excitement in the air. I'm always more motivated, as it's always so worthwhile to work hard for the experience of the Olympics. It's an amazing feeling to belong among the top German athletes and to compete for my country at the biggest sporting event in the world.

# Diversified Training
## — For Every Horse

# Objectives and Benefits

*A solid and versatile basic training is the foundation on which I build everything else. Ensuring diversified training for all my horses in their daily work — in addition to their basic training — lies near and dear to my heart.*

For my event horses that are expected to shine in every discipline, it's important to keep them fit in all three disciplines: dressage, cross-country, and show-jumping. And, why shouldn't my dressage horses share the enjoyment of training in an open field or experience the benefits of gymnastic jumping, such as loosening and strengthening their back muscles? Even my dressage stallion Franziskus is always super enthusiastic when jumping is part of his training plan. It's clear by the look in his eye that he is having fun with it and concentrating hard. Of course, I do not expect my dressage horses to complete a demanding cross-country course, just as I wouldn't expect my event horses to do much dressage at the Grand Prix level — the training is tailored to the individual horse, and his talents should be developed.

*Enjoying some downtime after work is done.*

*Cavalletti training.*

*Jumping.*

What training should never be is one-sided or overwhelming. The main objective is to ensure the well-being and overall health and soundness of the horse. She who trains her horse for versatility and diversification from the beginning will quickly recognize his strengths and weaknesses, and can choose a discipline based on her horse's talents. Not every horse is suitable for every activity — a fact the rider must accept for the well-being of the animal.

In the following chapter, you will see which benefits each of the training components offers. The goal of a diversified training plan is to seek out exactly what the horse is best suited for among the wide variety of activities. For example, if at the beginning of training, you find your horse is somewhat tight in his back and riding him long and low does not loosen him up effectively, you can include the targeted use of cavalletti to help the horse find his natural rhythm and relax through his body at the same time. Dressage-oriented work out on the hills is also good for the dressage horse, so he can learn to move with better balance.

To shape a training plan that is richly diversified and emphasizes versatility, I build the following elements into the training of all of my horses, no matter their specialized discipline:

— Dressage work
— Cavalletti training
— Gymnastic jumping
— Hill work
— Hacking out

*Ears pricked forward while heading uphill.*

# Elements of Dressage Training

*On the following pages, I have laid out for you a few of the most important building blocks for dressage work. This chapter is structured around the flow of an imaginary schooling session, and has not been tailored toward the individual age or training level of the horse.*

## Goal of Training

First and foremost, we train to ensure long-term soundness in the horse. My goal is a motivated horse, who responds as much as possible to invisible, sensitive aids and moves forward of his own accord. I would like the horse to become more beautiful and impressive-looking as a result of being ridden correctly. When that's the case, I'm on the right path. Basic training in dressage, in accordance with the fundamentals of classical riding, is the essential foundation of this. Every specialized discipline out there, whether show-jumping, dressage, or competing at the highest levels of eventing, is built upon this foundation. Day to day, I take exactly the amount of time for training that an individual horse needs. This can vary greatly from horse to horse.

## The Rider's Seat

The rider also needs to work steadily on improving her seat and refining her aids. Without a correct seat, it is impossible to give the correct aids and, therefore, also impossible to train the horse correctly. It's essential that the rider's body has a supple engagement — a seat that is too loose is just as ineffective as a stiff, tense body position. The center is the so-called neutral pelvis. This is the key point of connection between horse and rider. A rider must be able to remain supple and relaxed while following the horse's movement from this point in order to be able to sit in balance.

From this neutral pelvis, lifts a quiet, straight upper body, the main task of which is to keep the rider's center of gravity in harmony with the horse's. Excessive movement of the upper body should be avoided.

When the upper body falls in front of or behind the vertical, the horse can lose his balance and the flow of his movement is compromised. One often sees this at the canter when the rider should be swinging with her seat to support the driving aids. Only a quiet and balanced upper body allows the rider's hands to be carried well and the achievement of a trusting connection with the horse's mouth.

The upright hands must remained closed; otherwise, the wrist cannot remain supple enough to turn the hand in or out as needed to facilitate give and take on the reins. Likewise, a supple following in the direction of the horse's mouth becomes impossible when the hands are open. Often, you will see the hands held at different heights, or flat hands that the rider is not really holding in position; this also hinders a consistent connection and soft contact with the horse's mouth.

The rider's legs should emerge from her hips and lie supplely against the horse's sides. The knee lies against the tack, but should never grip. Otherwise, the rider will essentially be lifting herself out of the saddle and it will be totally impossible to maintain a deep, following seat. The rider's legs surround the horse's trunk in a natural way, with the lower leg flat against the horse's side and the inside of the calves in constant contact with the horse. This allows for the rider to react in the right moment, driving forward with more or less pressure, or in the case of lateral movements, to either send the horse sideways or regulate his sideways movement.

*A balanced and supple seat with straight line from shoulder, hip, to heel.*

A word about the driving aids: it's important for the horse to react to the driving aids and go forward. Your legs cannot be clamped on for this. Most of the time, the rider's calf guides the movement of the horse with light pressure. If the horse loses impulsion or needs to be more forward, the leg can temporarily apply firmer pressure. The goal is for the horse to be sensitive to evermore refined aids. The more balanced and supple the rider's seat, the better she can give aids that are refined and precise.

## The Rider's Aids

The rider's three main aids are weight, leg, and rein. A good rider shows herself by being able to apply the aids "with feel." This means, she is positioned to give all the aids precisely and in coordination with one another.

The rider applies the weight aids by the smallest shifting of her weight, and as such, her center of gravity. We distinguish between weighting both seat bones evenly, weighting one side or lightening the seat. Moving with the horse's body is always essential. I apply evenly weighted seat bones during a half-halt, for example, during a transition between the gaits, and during a full halt. To do so, I tip my pelvis a bit toward the back, make my seat bones heavy, and engage my abdominal and lower back muscles.

To lighten the weight aids, the rider takes her weight slightly forward, though the seat stays in the saddle. Her body position follows the horse's forward movement and her center of gravity shifts forward slightly. The lightened seat aids should be noticeable to the horse, but invisible to the onlooker. This is important during the warm-up phase and in gymnastic work as a release of the weighted seat aids, and to support forward movement, such as in extended trot or canter.

Weighting one side of the seat supports the horse's flexion and bend on a bending line. I use this to initiate and ride through turns and to influence the direction of the horse's movement. Here, I shift my weight more onto the inside seat bone. This causes my inside knee to lower a bit and my outside shoulder to come a bit more forward.

Leg aids encourage the horse to move more forward and/or sideways. Therefore, we distinguish between forward-driving, forward-sideways driving, and guarding (or regulating) leg aids. The forward-driving leg lies at or just behind the girth. The forward-sideways driving leg is taken back a bit farther, so that the forward-driving function remains in place as this is happening. This aid supports the flexion and bending and allows the horse to step forward and sideways with his inside hind as necessary for lateral movements. The guarding outside leg lies a bit behind the girth. It supports the activity of the

*Weighting one side of the seat on a bending line.*

*Weight, leg, and rein aids are coordinated precisely with one another.*

hind legs. On bending lines, the guarding outside leg prevents the horse's hindquarters from drifting to the outside. It ensures the horse moves forward evenly onto both reins.

Rein aids are always given in combination with weight and leg aids. I use them for all half-halts, that is, during transitions from one gait to another, as well as for full halts, preparation for a new movement, or to improve the connection. It's only possible to give a rein aid with feel when I have a balanced and supple seat. With rein aids, we also distinguish between a yielding rein, an asking rein, a non-yielding rein, and an opening rein. After every asking or non-yielding rein aid, a yielding rein aid must follow. An asking rein aid should be given with feel from a supple wrist. It should only last a moment and must be followed by a yielding rein. A give and take on the reins must always work together and be followed by the other. The connection with the horse's mouth must never become fixed, but rather must remain soft and elastic. The opening rein aid should be given with the inside hand and guides the horse through the turn. This aid is always combined with a slight shifting of the rider's weight.

Across the board, it's important to ensure that all three riding aids are used in conjunction with one another and to remember they cannot be applied in isolation from one another.

*Rein aids must be given with feel from a supple wrist.*

# The Warm-Up Phase

*Take enough time to warm up and come together with your partner. This goes for horses of any age and is important both physically and mentally.*

## Time to Warm Up

No matter how old the horse is or how far along he may be in his training, every schooling session begins with an extensive "loosening phase." Actually, the term "warm-up phase" is better in this context: when the right management approach is in place, including time to unwind and regular turn-out, the horse should not really show any signs of tension needing to be loosened as he begins his work. On the contrary, the point is to bring the horse's body temperature up to a "working temperature."

Tendons and ligaments need to be warmed up for at least 10 – 15 minutes at the walk, in order for them to get supple. Also, the synovial fluid responsible for lubricating the joints needs this time to get flowing enough to really protect the joints. The heart rate and circulatory system must gain momentum. Therefore, any rider who cares about the soundness of her horse will not cut this time short. It is only after 15 – 20 minutes of warm-up that you can expect and ask for optimal performance of the horse's body. In the warm-up phase, the goal should be for the horse to stretch extensively, long and low. He should lower his neck, trustingly seeking contact and chew the reins out of the rider's hand.

## Ride Long Enough at Walk

For all of the reasons named above, it is important to begin work by first riding at least 10 minutes at the walk on a loose rein. On relaxed and quiet horses, the reins can be on held on the buckle. With horses that can still be a bit fresh at the start of work, I ride on the longest rein possible. At the same time, I give through my elbows to allow the horse's neck to move up and down freely, so as not to jeopardize the quality of the walk. In addition, the warm-up phase allows both the horse and rider to prepare mentally for the ride to come. For this, a minimum of 10 minutes at the walk is needed. In order to truly get a feel for how long this takes, every rider should subtly take a look at her watch as she begins her ride. She can use this time to let go of the stress

*Riding at the walk on a long rein is the beginning of every warm-up phase.*

of the day, really tuning in and getting focused on her horse. At my place, we usually warm up by walking once or twice around the track that surrounds our pastures.

With some horses, it can be advisable to already think about getting them to chew the reins out of the hand at the walk. In this time, the rider attempts to use half-halts to encourage the horse to lower his poll a bit deeper.

## Loosening at the Trot

After loosening up at the walk, the rider slowly takes the reins and begins a diligent working trot. At the posting trot, it is important to make sure that the horse is not coming behind the bit, but rather is actually stretching and being sent forward by the rider. Through the combination of the driving aids and an appropriately soft hand that repeatedly touches the horse's mouth, the horse will be induced to seek and maintain a contact with the bit.

Especially with horses that yield very easily at the poll, you must really make sure they are not becoming too tight, and instead encourage them to seek a deeper connection. At the same time, the horse should be striking off actively with his hind legs, with a relaxed back, and with his neck being allowed to stretch down from his withers. It is a complete error to pull the horse's head down with the hand. When this takes place, the horse will round his neck but will quickly end up behind the vertical and blocked through his back. It is impossible to develop an honest connection and throughness with willing cooperation in this way. You'll quickly see the result — a tight horse that moves without rhythm. It's therefore extremely important to support the horse with half-halts as he seeks a long and low connection.

*Loosening at the posting trot: The horse trots with relaxation and seeks a long and low connection.*

# Establishing Rhythm

At the beginning of the warm-up phase, I make sure to establish and maintain my horse's rhythm. As part of rhythm, you are looking for symmetry at the walk, trot, and canter. I concentrate on making sure I do not disturb the horse's movement and influence him with feel.

# Balance

When I ride my horse in accordance with the steps of the Training Scale, his balance improves automatically. The matter of balance is important at every step of training, from the very beginning on, and is directly connected with rhythm. Relaxation with suppleness also plays a role. The more relaxed and supple my horse is, the better he can balance himself.

# Riding on the Circle

In the loosening phase, it's important that my horse lets go of any tension and relaxes. Signs of relaxation with suppleness include a swinging back, a peaceful facial expression, chewing on the bit, a loosely held tail that swings like a pendulum, and blowing through the nose. In addition, as the rider allows the horse to chew the reins from her hands, the horse's neck should come farther forward and downward. When trotting on a bending line, the horse must be flexing and bending to the inside. I ride mainly on circles and, of course, in both directions.

I turn onto the circle by softly turning in my inside hand and then giving again. The horse should flex to the inside and give. My inside leg comes just slightly behind the girth, with the inside of my calf flat against the horse's side. This leg drives the horse onto the outside rein and in doing so, encourages the horse to bend. So, the diagonal aids are employed. As this takes place, the outside rein stays quietly on and serves to establish an outside boundary. The outside rein stays straight, keeps a quiet contact with the horse's mouth and allows the flexion, while at the same time, the inside hand repeatedly guides the head and neck to the inside and, in doing so, asks for the flexion.

The rider should continually try to improve the positioning and bending with the use of repeated half-halts. Always, if the rider establishes the desired give from the horse in the desired direction, she should bring the hand slightly forward thus showing the horse he is on the right track. Every time the horse gives through the neck, a give on the rein is the reward. Gradually, many small half-halts guide the horse to stretch long and low. When the horse is concentrating well on the circle, I can try using the whole arena in order to see if the rhythm is

*Allowing the horse to chew the reins out of the rider's hands on a circle.*

maintained on straight lines. On the straight sides of the whole arena, always think about lengthening the trot stride, so that the horse trots diligently enough.

If the horse tries to come up out of his long and low frame, the rider must react as quickly as possible. She should resist his attempt, drive him forward and then give again, if possible not waiting until the horse has really got his neck and head up high but rather reacting at the first signs of this.

Some horses tend to get distracted at the same spot over and over again. In such situations, it's advisable to keep him in this place (perhaps riding him in shoulder-in past the "dangerous" spot) until the excitement passes. Frequent changes of direction are important in order to supple the horse on both sides. If the horse should continue to allow himself to be distracted by the environment, ride along quietly and calmly until the horse lets go of this tension.

## Serpentines

Three-loop serpentines using the whole arena are a great exercise for the warm-up phase, as they allow the horse to relax through his rib cage and foster lateral bend. From the beginning, the rider must make sure that the horse is clearly repositioned as he crosses the centerline on each loop. In doing so, the new inside leg must really come through, meaning the rider must again drive the horse into the newly established outside rein and not allow him to fall out through his shoulder. During the work phase, the number of serpentines can increase. I always ride round serpentines during training, so that I can more clearly apply my inside leg and supple the inside ribs. I make sure to ride each loop very precisely.

# Loosening at Canter

Trot-canter transitions are an important element of the warm-up phase, and I practice them again and again.

Some horses relax more easily at canter than at trot. The rider canters on a circle, driving with the inside leg and attempts, through half-halting and repeatedly giving the reins forward, to ride the horse in a long and low, stretchy frame. The rider must be patient and wait for the horse to trust her enough to stretch his neck forward and downward from the withers and to give through his back.

Initially, the rider will still sit lightly in this phase and, even better, take a light seat in order to unburden the horse's back and communicate to the horse that he can trust himself more to seek out long and low. *Überstreichen* (releasing the contact completely) and *vorfühlen* (a slight give forward within the contact) are great ways to build his trust in this process. As soon as the horse is relaxed while cantering on the circle, I ride the whole arena and can lengthen the canter stride on the long sides.

After some time at the canter, I can again transition down to the trot and ride on in a diligent working tempo. The horse should have a quiet tail, a soft mouth, and attentive ears — these are all signals for the beginning of relaxation with suppleness. It's now very important to

*Loose at the canter: the horse stretches trustfully into the hand.*

allow the horse to chew the reins from your hands. The horse should seek his way toward long and low and trustingly stretch into the hand. Thereby, the rider must drive him on and ride forward, as Paul Stecken emphasizes. Allowing the horse to chew the reins out of the hand without having him move diligently forward at the same time is useless.

## Encourage Supple Relaxation

Throughout the entire loosening phase, it's important to work on the horse's *Losgelassenheit* (supple relaxation). By supple relaxation, we understand that the engagement and relaxation of the horse's musculature occurs without physical tension and with the horse remaining calm internally as well. Trot-canter transitions are important exercises of the warm-up phase, as they help the horse achieve supple relaxation. I can quietly ride several transitions until the horse is happily blowing out through his nose and loosely swinging through his back while maintaining an even tempo and seeking long and low.

## Establishing Connection

The more quietly both hands remain over the withers, the more quiet the connection will be and the horse can trustfully seek and maintain contact. We talk about how the connection is truly established when there is a light, steady contact between the rider's hand and the horse's mouth. This ideal can only occur when the rider is sitting in balance at all times, a prerequisite for a quiet hand.

It's a known fact that the warm-up phase should last as long as it takes for the horse to truly relax and no longer be holding any tension. Loosening the back is essential! Give your horse the time he needs. You'll be rewarded for your patience in the work phase. Upon completion of the loosening work, a walk break on a loose rein always follows.

**FOR EVERY HORSE:**
A walk break on a loose rein comes in between the warm-up phase and work phase.

*A tail swinging quietly, like a pendulum...*

*... is a sign of supple relaxation.*

*Franziskus is happy to practice flying changes in an open field.*

# The Work Phase

*Based on your horse's level of training, determine the demands and goals for this training session. Always end the work phase with a positive experience and in a positive state of mind.*

## Set Concrete Goals

While the warm-up and cool-down phases will always look quite similar, the content of the working session depends, of course, on what the rider would like to train the horse to do. Use the principle of going from easy to difficult to build your work phase, or from known exercises to new material. Set a definite goal for what you want to work toward in the session, and then ride exercises appropriate for the age and training level of your horse. Even with this in mind, you should make sure not to exceed the time frame you have set for the work phase (usually about 25 – 30 minutes), which can also mean that you have to scale back your own ambition in order to avoid overwhelming the horse.

Plan ahead as to what you would like to train in this session, but always monitor the actual circumstances and situations that present themselves. Organization is an important part of successful training, but we are working with a living creature and should always take the horse's needs into consideration. Pay attention to your horse's status on any given day and work with what is. A good rider knows her horse and should always be willing and able to react with flexibility, alongside her planning. For example, here too, it can also be a matter of adjusting your training to suit the weather: taking too long a walk break in cold weather can be just as unhealthy as working the horse too strenuously during intense heat.

I like to complete my dressage training in an open field or ride some dressage exercises during hill work. However, when training out in the open, the rider should always take the general conditions of the footing into consideration.

## Walk Breaks

Regular breaks should also be built into the work phase. This time gives your horse the chance to recover physically, relax mentally, and process whatever you are working on. In addition, regular breaks to recover are not only important for the horse, but also for the rider. She can also use the breaks to reflect on the work up to that point and to think about how to proceed further with the training.

It is important to concentrate during training, for the rider just as much as the horse; however, neither should be overworked or overwhelmed. Regular walk breaks are also a part of the work phase, and I also build them in as a reward after a well-done exercise. Variety is equally important: constant repetition of a particular demand at one time should be avoided. Over time, this will only lead to boredom or can cause stress to build up. Always build in diverse variations and then turn back to the desired request.

## Find a Good Stopping Point

The working phase should always be concluded after the horse performs positively. Toward the end of this phase, ask your horse to perform a task that you know he will execute very well and then end by praising your horse extensively. This way, you can transition happily into the cool-down phase. This is the easiest way to ensure the horse maintains motivation and has fun while working, and that he will also begin his training in a positive frame of mind the next day.

*It's motivating to end on a good note.*

# The Trot

*Following the walk break at the end of the warm-up phase, I begin the work phase by carefully taking up the reins and beginning to sit the trot. With a sensitive fine-tuning of the aids, I now activate the horse's hindquarters.*

Now, my objective is for the horse to go in definite self-carriage, with his nose ahead of the vertical. This means he carries his head and neck himself, at the appropriate placement for his level of training. The poll is the highest point. Even the young horses learn quickly: warm-up phase means posting trot and traveling long and low, while the work phase means sitting trot and self-carriage. To be honest, I also have to admit that along the way to this ideal, there will always be situations

*This trot shows lots of impulsion, and a quiet, steady connection.*

where the connection must be a little stronger or the horse comes behind the vertical. Through the sensitive application of the aids, it's absolutely necessary to quickly find a way to improve the situation. First and foremost, it is important to strive for a connection where the rider feels a light pressure, meaning comfortable and even.

## Elevation

The concept of "elevation" is closely related to collection. The more elevated the horse is, meaning he's enlarged and lifted the entire forehand including shoulder, neck, and head, the more he must develop flexion in

*The horse shifts the weight onto his hindquarters and moves in a lovely self-carriage.*

the major joints of his hindquarters. This means the horse must learn to lower his hindquarters in order to shift weight onto them and, in doing so, lighten the forehand. This allows him the possibility to open up, moving more freely, bigger and more expressively.

It's a given that a young horse is not yet able to carry himself in a highly elevated frame, as his muscles, tendons, and ligaments are not yet developed to that point. Therefore, we also speak here of "relative" elevation, relative in relationship from forehand to hindquarters. "Absolute" elevation is incorrect and describes a higher carriage of head and neck that is forced from the rider's hands.

## Half-Halts

For me, the half-halt is the most important tool for fine-tuning the horse. I always need one if I want to take my horse's attention to something new, such as a new exercise, a change in tempo, or when approaching a new jump cross-country or in stadium. I also give a half-halt to prepare the horse for a transition from one gait to another, or to regulate the tempo within a gait. Half-halts are essential for reaching and improving self-carriage and collection. The half-halt is the most subtle sign that I can give a horse — it's whispering with the horse.

When riding a half-halt, the rider must always understand the interplay between her weight, leg, and rein aids. This means, she engages abdominal and back muscles (weight aids), adds pressure to the quiet leg that lies against the horse's side (leg aids), and at the same time holds lightly on the reins, then with feel gives with the hand (rein aids). A half-halt only lasts about two seconds (or less). I therefore must give my aids very quickly and in tune with one another.

## "Throughness" with Willing Cooperation

The beginning of *Durchlässigkeit* (throughness with willing cooperation) is continually developed in the course of the horse's education and training. The more educated the horse, the more through he will become. Throughness refers to the horse accepting the rider's aids with willing cooperation, motivation, and relaxation, so that the impulsion from the hindquarters travels diligently through the horse's body, and returns with flow to the rider's hand. A sensitive fine-tuning of the aids is very important to achieving throughness with willing cooperation.

**HALF-HALTS**
"Every half-halt ends with a give to the horse."

**COMMUNICATION**
"The half-halt must always be more interesting than the environment."
Paul Stecken

*Trot-walk transitions are even more valuable when ridden on the line of a circle, as they also improve the lateral bend.*

# Transitions

The first exercise on the way to throughness with willing cooperation is trot-walk transitions. Within the concept of throughness, it is understood the horse must remain relaxed and supple while responding obediently to driving aids from seat and leg, as well as to restraining or non-yielding rein aids. Transitions between trot and walk improve throughness while simultaneously encouraging the horse to activate his hindquarters. This is the horse's motor, both the source of impulsion at first and of the increased carrying power later required to develop collection.

When a young horse is first learning the exercise, I allow myself one to two horse length's time to execute a quiet transition, and I use my voice to support the downward transition. Half-halts prepare the horse for the exercise. To execute this, I engage my lower back and apply both legs evenly while taking contact on both reins. I give again immediately, as soon as I feel the horse respond to the aids. As this takes place, the horse may lift out of the contact or lean on the rider's hands. I prevent this by repeatedly taking contact and giving again as we trot forward energetically. The walk-trot transitions are an indicator as to whether the horse is truly on the aids. The control of the poll remains steady and the contact is consistent.

Later, I ride trot-walk transitions with just one walk stride in order to improve the liveliness of the horse's strike-off with the hind legs. The hindquarters should begin to carry more weight and track up under the horse's center of gravity, which, in turn, develops the carrying power of the hindquarters. It is important the transitions are ridden smoothly and with the use of refined aids, without halting.

# Impulsion

After successful transitions in both directions, during which I've improved the carrying power of the hindquarters by giving half-halts with feel, I always ride the horse forward. After collecting with the transitions, I must always ride the horse forward with impulsion. Within the concept of impulsion, we understand the power from the hindquarters carries forth over the horse's swinging back as his entire movement is directed forward. Impulsion also shows itself in a more pronounced moment of suspension. Therefore, trot and canter rank among the gaits with impulsion, but not the walk.

A horse is trotting or cantering with impulsion when he strikes off energetically with his hind foot and swings significantly forward with his hind legs during the moment of suspension. Impulsion is most visible at the extended gaits. Systematically developed impulsion is visible in the horse's joyful way of going. Transitions are an important

**IMPULSION**

By riding transitions correctly and fluidly, I can develop impulsion by adding and capturing it.

*Adding to the trot stride...*                    *...and reducing it with feel.*

part of this: a trot and canter with impulsion must be developed. Bolting forward suddenly or faltering abruptly do not encourage quality of movement.

After riding voltes or serpentines, it's again important to pick up impulsion. Paul Stecken says, "Serpentines with five loops down and back—then you'll get results." Afterward, I lengthen the trot in order to feel the horse move relaxed through his rib cage and step better behind. After all this, if the back is supple and the nose is ahead of the vertical, then his hind legs can really engage.

## Beginning to Cross Over

I can first get the horse used to the aids for lateral movements at the walk, in that I begin to ask him to cross over with his legs on the "open side" of a circle, that is, the half of the circle nearest to the center of the arena (the "closed side" is the half of the circle closest to the arena wall). I bring the forehand to the inside, as if I were going to ride a volte, but apply my inside leg and a quiet outside rein, trying repeatedly, step by step, to encourage the horse to cross over with his legs. The horse is positioned to the inside as this takes place.

Before I attempt this cross over with my horse at the trot, he needs to have understood the aids. When this exercise works well at the walk, I try the same thing at the trot. After he crosses over for half a circle, I again post the trot and stop asking him to cross over, picking up the impulsion and getting the horse in front of my driving aids once again. Now, I change directions, transition down to the walk, and start over again on the new side. Frequent changes of direction in every element of training improve the even gymnastic effect on both sides of the horse's body. This is an essential prerequisite for straightness, another important training goal.

## Straightness

The goal of straightness is to correct the horse's naturally occurring asymmetries and maintain suppleness on both sides of the body. A straight horse is then able to move in balance with the forehand and hindquarters on a single track, whether traveling on straight or bending lines. He allows himself to be flexed and bent well, and moves evenly into both reins. He is equally good at turning and approaching jumps in either direction.

The riding of bending lines develops straightness. When rhythm, supple relaxation, connection, and impulsion have been achieved, the "bending work for straightening" can follow with the incorporation of voltes, half-pirouettes at the walk, serpentines, and exercises such as shoulder-fore and shoulder-in.

## Lateral Movements

Lateral movements such as shoulder-in, haunches-in, haunches-out, and half-pass are not in and of themselves the end goal; rather, they are exercises ridden with even lateral bend, which work in conjunction with one another to straighten the horse. Straightening work plays an important, deciding role in the horse's education. It's the key to evenly

*Shoulder-fore, but the poll should be higher!*

"gymnasticizing" both sides of the horse's body. Only in this way will the horse use his body in balance and remain sound. Lateral movements make an important contribution to this effort.

These exercises require well-coordinated use of the diagonal aids: the weight is shifted somewhat to the inside as the inside leg just behind the girth sends the horse forward into a guarding outside leg and rein. The inside rein positions the horse. When referring to the "inside" in terms of lateral movements, we are always talking about the "hollow" side, that is, the direction in which the horse is bent.

## Riding with Flexion

When riding with flexion, the horse is positioned to the inside without his forehand coming off the track. The hind legs get the signal to step significantly smaller. The outside hind leg lands between the tracks of the two front legs. Riding with flexion is one of the important preparatory exercises for later riding haunches-in, haunches-out, and half-pass.

## Shoulder-Fore

In the beginning with an unschooled horse, crossing over with the legs should only be asked as a shoulder-fore. In other words, there's a hint of shoulder-in, but ridden with much less longitudinal bend than the shoulder-in. The horse is encouraged to step a bit smaller with his hind legs. The requests made of a young horse should always be broken down into steps, so that he does not become overwhelmed while he is learning. The rider can imagine that she's riding the horse straight ahead, but with a longitudinal bend. Shoulder-fore is a movement that promotes collection.

## Shoulder-In

Shoulder-in is one of the most important movements in the pursuit of dressage, as it brings together many gymnastic elements. Shoulder-in requires the inside hind to step farther under the horse's center of gravity, which, in turn, improves the flexion of the hindquarters and the horse's ability to collect. At the same time, the shoulder becomes much freer, which allows the development of more impulsion in the horse's movement.

When executing shoulder-in, the forehand comes off the rail, toward the inside of the arena. The horse is bent evenly and his hind end travels almost straight down the track. Only his forelegs should cross and the movement should be ridden at an approximately 30-degree angle. Over time, the shoulder-in should develop so that you can ride it at a very constant angle. When viewed from the front, the horse should be seen

*Shoulder-in ridden with correct angle.*

71

moving on three tracks, meaning the outside front leg and the inside hind are moving on the same track.

## Haunches-In (Travers)

Whereas with shoulder-in the forehand leads by coming off the rail, it is the hindquarters that come to the inside for haunches-in. The forehand stays on the rail. Haunches-in can be initiated effectively when coming out of a corner. The rider first gives a half-halt, then shortens the inside rein and shifts her weight somewhat to the inside seat bone; at the same time, the inside leg remains just behind the girth and is responsible for keeping the bend and the forward drive of the inside hind, and the outside leg lies behind the girth in a guarding position and drives the horse sideways. The inside hand positions the horse, maybe through a slight opening rein, and the outside rein gives lightly, allowing the positioning to the inside, even as it simultaneously limits the horse on the outside.

Haunches-in can also be initiated effectively by performing a volte halfway down the long side, then carrying the positioning and bend with you as you continue farther down the long side. In haunches-in, the horse travels on four distinct tracks, and both the fore and hind legs should cross distinctly and evenly.

## Half-Pass

Subsequently, you can also ride the first half-passes from the centerline out. It's advisable to lead in to the half-pass from a light shoulder-in, as doing so helps to prevent the hindquarters from leading.

*01 Distinct crossing of the front legs in half-pass to the left.*

*02 Crossing the hind legs in half-pass to the left.*

*01*  *02*

In half-pass to the left, the horse is positioned to the left. Then, you initiate the sideways movement by shifting your weight to the left and applying your right leg, driving sideways. The left leg drives from just behind the girth and is responsible for maintaining bend in the direction of movement. In the beginning, a few steps are enough. It is important that the forehand always leads and the horse moves forward energetically after the half-pass. The crossing of fore and hind legs must be clearly recognizable. Important characteristics of the half-pass include cadence and a consistent flow in the movement. Naturally, the benefits of lateral movements are only present when they are practiced evenly on both sides. With young horses, lateral movements should only be ridden for short amounts of time.

## Lengthening Strides

Lengthening work at the trot is both valuable and important, and should always be integrated in between lateral movements. Going into this, the rider needs to use half-halts to engage the hindquarters, loading the horse's body like a spring. By driving the horse more and sending the hands forward, energy is produced that can then be released into ground-covering strides that are full of impulsion and yet controlled.

When lengthening the stride across the diagonal, it's important to make sure the horse is loose through his back and maintains his rhythm. When the horse tenses up, the rider will notice immediately, as she will find it more difficult to sit the horse's trot. In this case, it is advisable to continue lengthening the trot across the diagonal, but in posting trot. This should activate the hind legs and, by doing so, relieve the tension in the horse's back. In the corner, the horse should be brought back noticeably. Then, the rider can again try sitting the trot across the diagonal.

## Medium Trot

To maintain impulsion, try this exercise: first half-pass to the centerline, then straighten the horse and continue along the centerline, preferably at posting trot. And the other way around: first ride down the long side and then carry the impulsion with you as you half-pass to the centerline.

The goal of trot lengthenings is the medium trot or extended trot, respectively. Here, you really need to pay attention to riding the horse evenly on both reins and keeping him straight. The ground cover will increase through the powerful thrust of the hindquarters and the forehand swinging through freely. The horse should remain in self-carriage even as he covers distinctly more ground and should come a bit farther in front of the vertical. The poll is the highest point.

*Good freedom through the shoulder while half-passing to the left.*

*Medium trot across the diagonal with good self-carriage.*

*Clear lowering of the hindquarters during transition to halt.*

*Standing square.*

## Executing the Full Halt

The aids for a full halt should always bring the horse to a complete standstill. With young horses, you practice this from the walk or trot. Horses are prepared for a full halt with one or more half-halts. In the beginning with young horses, you calmly allow two or three strides to complete the halt and support the horse with the voice. Once the horse has halted, the asking rein aid must immediately stop and the hand must become soft, so the horse does not drop behind the vertical and hide behind the bridle. From the beginning on, the horse must become accustomed to standing as evenly as possible on all four legs for at least four to five seconds without moving. As this takes place, your seat relaxes but you are still in contact with the horse with all your aids. In this way, you can immediately correct a head toss or backward step, for example. As soon as the horse has understood the exercise, there should no longer be intermediary steps of walk as he transitions to halt.

In the beginning, I practice trot-walk-halt with contact along the rail, then later on open lines. With more advanced horses, I also train the full halt from the canter. In dressage tests, the halt comes right at the beginning after you enter the arena on the centerline and salute the judges, and it is required again at the close of the test. Therefore, I practice riding up the centerline in trot or canter and halting straight and completely at X. This is a rider's first impression on the judge — her "business card," if you will.

In order to be able to give the correct aids and execute the full halt, the rider must have a balanced seat. Breathing in deeply allows the vertebrae to straighten elastically, as an uninhibited leg surrounds the horse's body and the independent hand provides resistance, but lightly. This must all happen in the correct sequence and in a fluid movement.

# Standing at the Halt

It's important a horse can stand quietly: in fact, he should learn the word "halt" means to stop — standing still, pausing for moment, sustaining his halt, and remaining relaxed. Nervous or insecure horses by nature find this difficult, but it is exactly these horses that will enhance their inner strength by mastering this exercise.

Standing at the halt is a fundamental exercise in my daily training. Even the young horses learn to remain standing for a couple of seconds. I frame them with my weight, leg and rein aids, which provide them the security they need to stay standing. The horses remain standing until I tell them they can move on. They must wait for a signal from me and only then can they trot on. I do not accept the horse deciding of his own accord to move on. In the beginning, I keep the horse standing only as long as I believe he can tolerate it, and that is decided based on the individual. It's important that I ride on before the horse takes over that decision.

*The young horse learns to remain standing for several moments.*

*An obedient halt — straight and square.*

Halting is an exercise in both obedience and relaxation, as well as a dressage movement. Standing completely still at the halt is always a sign of true relaxation. Of course, the horse must learn to stand straight and square, but sustaining the exercise is really first and foremost a test of patience. So far, every horse I've trained has learned this exercise, including the "hot" horses and Thoroughbred types. Trained with perseverance, regular repetition, and consistency, the halt belongs among the mandatory requirements for my horses. When competing, I'm so very pleased each time my dressage test concludes and I can give the judges a final salute while my horse stands quietly, chewing the reins from my hands, and then, with my signal, remain relaxed as he leaves the dressage arena.

# Rein-Back

Rein-back is a demanding exercise for the horse, as it is a collected exercise where the legs move in diagonal pairs. Rein-back can help to test and improve throughness with willing cooperation, collection, and obedience. Prerequisites for this movement include that there is already a known degree of willing cooperation and that the full halt from walk and trot are being performed reliably. To ride the rein-back, you need a combination of seat, leg, and rein aids. The horse should remain straight, square, and on the bridle. Then, I give him the same weight and leg aids as I would to ask him to move forward. As soon as the horse begins to step forward, I immediately apply a light asking rein aid, which prompts the horse to step backward, moving his legs in diagonal pairs. In the beginning, the legs stay back a bit in a warning position and, when needed, can correct the tendency of the horse to

*Standing quietly and square before the rein-back.*

*Rein-back with diagonal steps.*

become crooked while backing. In time, the rein aids can become more and more refined. For horses with weak backs, you can make the rein-back easier to perform by avoiding sitting too heavily in the saddle, and instead tilting forward lightly toward the front.

As a general rule, the rein-back is exercised for one horse-length, meaning about two or three strides. I make sure that it is at least four strides and the halt afterward is square.

## Collection

The older, more mature, and further along in his education that a horse is, the more he must collect himself. By the term collection, it is understood the horse is shifting more of his own and his rider's weight onto his haunches, which happens through a deeper flexion of the three large joints of his hindquarters: the hip, the stifle, and the hock. In everyday terms, this is described as lowering and engaging the hindquarters. By gymnasticizing the tendons and ligaments and developing the relevant musculature, the horse will be more able to "sit," as we say. Consequently, he will shift his center of gravity and can move more freely and more elevated up front. With his hindquarters coming more underneath him, the horse can step more lightly and energetically, raising himself more in self-carriage. Collection is not achieved by a backward-pulling hand, but rather must originate from the seat and accompanying driving aids.

*The piaffe can also be done in an open field.*

## Cadence

At advanced levels of training, the concept of cadence comes more and more into effect. Cadence means that the moment of suspension in the movement is held longer and is more pronounced. As this takes place, the hind legs must step up powerfully and energetically, definitely swinging through toward the front end, and causing the movement to become more elevated and expressive. When this doesn't happen with the hindquarters, the rider will get an erroneous, exaggerated movement of the forelegs, which can certainly appear spectacular, but is being generated from a tense and tightly held back. This leads to physical damage.

For successful training, it is vital for the trainer to note when the horse begins to lose endurance and power. An exercise should end before the horse reaches this point and while he is still working willingly. Consider those all-important walk breaks, which are especially needed right after strenuous collected exercises.

# The Walk

*The walk is a four-beat gait. A ground-covering, rhythmic stride is a sure sign of a horse that is relaxed and supple. Every training session must include multiple walk breaks.*

Dressage distinguishes between the medium, extended, and collected walk. The medium walk is the equivalent of the working tempo for this gait. The horse's strides should be fresh, even, and unrestricted. The hind feet should reach a bit past the hoof print of the front feet with each stride.

*Relaxed walk on a long rein.*

At the extended walk, the horse steps with wide, ground-covering strides, which should be as long as his conformation allows. He must not be rushing. His hind feet now step clearly over the hoof print of the front feet. The rider allows the horse full freedom through the neck, but without giving up the connection to the horse's mouth, or the control of the poll.

At the collected walk, the height of the horse's neck corresponds to the level of collection he has achieved. Each individual stride covers less ground, and therefore, the hind feet preferably land in the hoof prints of the front feet. At the same time, the strides are more elevated, as the joints of the hindquarters must bend more deeply. Forward movement and rhythm must not be lost.

It's important for the rider to follow the bobbing movement of the horse's neck and head, maintaining soft elbows. This is especially true during transitions from trot to walk and canter to walk, where a timely following from the elbow joint determines whether a good walk will be immediately possible following the transition.

In my book *Basic Training of the Young Horse,* there is an entire chapter devoted to the walk, which explains all important steps specific to developing the walk in the young horse. For this reason, I have included here just three examples of exercises for the walk.

## Crossing Over at the Walk

At the walk, I can get the horse accustomed to the lateral aids by allowing him to cross over with his legs while on a circle. I turn the forehand in on the circle, as if I were going to ride a volte, then use my inside leg to send him toward a steady outside rein. As I do so, I try repeatedly, stride by stride, to encourage the horse to cross over with his legs. The horse is positioned to the inside throughout. Crossing over in this way develops suppleness and straightnesss.

*Crossing over on the open side of a circle.*

## Half-Pirouette

Next, I ride a clear and diligent medium walk. From the elbow, my hands follow the bobbing movement of the horse's neck. This is important as a rigid hand will block the walk. I find it best to first work in the half-pirouette on the track along the rail, so the horse has a good connection. It's definitive to the half-pirouette that the hind legs step evenly in a small half-circle. I begin the movement with a half-halt, then weight my inside seat bone and position the horse in the direction of travel. My inside leg is applied just behind the girth, while the outside leg lies in a guarding position behind the girth. The inside rein guides the horse into the turn, while the

*Half-pirouette: the horse turns on a small circle around the inside hind...*

*...the forelegs cross.*

outside rein gives just enough that the turn is possible and also limits the amount of bend.

On the first attempts, the circle on which the hind legs are moving can certainly be a bit larger but the biggest error is when the horse walks backward. If this exercise is going well along the rail, you can also try it on open lines. However, with some horses that tend to rely heavily on the rail for support, it may even be advisable to reverse this. Or, in the beginning, I just ride a quarter-pirouette. In this case, I ride a circle with corners and in each corner, I include a quarter-pirouette.

The turn should not be too rushed, or else the horse will tense up, step backward and/or barge through the turn. The rider should always think about initiating the exercise with feel for her horse and maintaining the walk rhythm, fluidity, and forward momentum. After the half-pirouette, you can execute a good upward transition to canter, as the half-pirouette will have brought the horse's hindquarters well underneath him, and he'll be prepared for an uphill transition into canter. The basis for this is that you can only work effectively on the

*A lovely collected canter, developed out of the half-pirouette.*

canter and collect the canter strides when the horse is truly in front of
the driving aids. Some changes in tempo while on a circle help with
this. You must make sure the horse reacts promptly and lightly.

## Walk Pirouettes

Next, I ride an extended walk, then transition to collected walk and
ride a pirouette on an open line somewhere in the arena. The aids for
the walk pirouette are the same as for the half-pirouette, except that
the full pirouette is ridden from a collected walk. With good contact
and a light longitudinal bend, the horse's forehand should describe a
circle around his hindquarters. The point of the turn lies as close as
possible to the inside hind foot, which lifts and lowers in accordance
with the walk rhythm. The outside hind makes a small half-circle
around the inside hind as the front legs step forward and sideways,
crossing. In contrast, the hind legs should not cross.

*I like to incorporate walk breaks as a reward after a challenging exercise.*

## Walk Breaks

Extended breaks at the walk serve as a recovery period after strenuous training sequences. Without these breaks, lactic acid builds up in the horse's muscles and they start to hurt. It's not uncommon for this to lead to resistance, which occurs suddenly and seemingly without reason. When the rider notices that the horse needs a break, she should first make sure that the horse is carrying himself. For example, on the open side of a circle, the rider puts both hands forward and momentarily releases the contact (*Überstreichen*), in order to check that the horse is correctly on the aids. If so, only then does she allow the horse to chew the reins out of her hands. If the horse does not come forward sufficiently with his nose, "getting stuck" as we say, the rider must continue riding until the horse trusts himself enough to truly reach long and low. The rider may need to explore, incorporating transitions, driving him forward and riding turns until she finds what works. This can sometimes take a while. Afterward, the horse should be rewarded with big pats on his neck and a lengthy walk break with the reins as long as possible.

# The Canter

*The movement in canter should be ground-covering and expansive. The horse lifts himself clearly off the ground and canters energetically forward and upward, with a loose back and lowered hindquarters.*

## Canter Departure from the Trot

With young horses, we initially practice canter departures from the trot. The best position for picking up the canter is the end of the open side of a circle, just before you return to the track. A half-halt prepares the horse for the transition, then you shift your weight to the inside while pressing the horse forward from your inside hip and really giving on your inside rein. Then, you can take your outside shoulder back a bit and take up the inside rein lightly. Finally, allow the first canter stride by energetically pushing forward with your inside seat bone as you engages through your back, drive forward from both legs and give with feeling from you inside hand.

With young horses, it does not always work right away and, as a rule, the left side is most often easier than the right due to natural asymmetry in the horse. If it does not work immediately, the horse must first be brought back to a calm and controlled trot, so that the canter transition can be attempted once again. The horse should be well-balanced at the canter, including on the bending line of a circle. The horse canters with a loose back, diligent tempo, quiet tail, happy eye, and softly chewing mouth. These are all signs of the horse's physical and mental relaxation.

After repeated practice on the circle, I ride the whole arena to open up the canter strides more freely. If the horse threatens to break, I repeat the aids as if I'd like to begin the canter again, which prevents him from feeling any uncertainty. Normally, however, the canter aids should not be repeated over and over again, as you want to the horse to learn to remain in canter of his own accord.

It's important to practice riding up a "free" line in the arena, from time to time. This means riding on a track several feet from the rail so that the horse learns to remain balanced without depending on the rail. I can also lengthen the canter strides some, but I really need to be cautious that when I bring the horse back, he does not break and transition down to the trot. When all this is working well, I can try to ride

*A canter transition on the circle in a jumping saddle.*

83

a single large volte in canter. This becomes the first attempt to induce the horse to step up more under his center of gravity, shifting more weight onto his hindquarters. This exercise is already moving carefully in the direction of collection.

## Canter Transition from the Walk

Crossing over is a good preparation for walk-to-canter transitions. The inside hind leg is activated, which helps to develop a good canter transition as well as improve the canter itself. The first canter transition from walk takes place on a circle. With younger horses, I initially need to be clearer and more definite with my aids: use half-halts, which position the horse slightly using the inside rein, weight in the inside stirrup, the outside leg coming back, and a little cluck of the tongue helping to support the driving aids.

If the horse lifts above the contact during the transition, you need to respond quickly to stop the horse's attempt as soon as it begins. It's crucial that you do not allow the horse to canter while he's above the contact, but rather when he yields again.

To summarize: Create clear positioning to the inside, think about crossing over — meaning the inside hind leg should have a hint of moving toward the outside, and transition to canter.

## Spiral In at Canter

An excellent exercise for improving the canter is spiraling in on a circle until it is the size of a volte. To do this, you should take your time on several rounds. It's especially important for more of the horse's weight to shift clearly onto the inside hind, and for the strides to be diligent and powerful. After a few rounds, transition down to the walk and back to the canter. These canter-walk transitions are an important preparation for flying-lead changes.

Now, gradually make the circle larger again by spiraling out and lengthening the canter strides. This can take place quietly over one or two rounds. If the horse tends to become too light in the contact during this exercise, it means the rider needs to drive more to improve the contact again. The rider must have the feeling that the horse is in front of her, not under her.

Spiraling in and out on a circle is a good exercise for working on the horse's throughness with willing cooperation.

*When spiraling out on a circle, I can lengthen the canter strides.*

*Notice how well my horse remains on the aids, even as I reach forward and release the contact (überstreichen) with my inside hand.*

## Simple Change of Lead

At first, the transition to walk is always conducted through the trot, until I can eliminate the trot strides altogether. I can practice canter-walk transitions really well by riding serpentines or a figure-eight on a circle. Each time I cross the centerline, I change the canter lead by executing a simple change. So, I have two 10-meter voltes on which the horse must collect himself nicely, and this improves lateral bend.

## Extending and Collecting the Canter Stride

After these exercises, it is high time to lengthen the canter stride down the long side. I ride in collected canter through the corner, direct my horse straight ahead and then develop the extended canter. On the

*Dynamic lengthening of the canter stride.*

long side, I can really gain momentum, regaining impulsion after the collected work. As I approach the corner, I collect my horse once again and then in the corner, I can reach forward once to momentarily release the contact. As momentum is added and then contained, my horse's throughness with willing cooperation becomes apparent, and his readiness for collection is developed.

## Counter-Canter

When the collected canter is truly balanced and my horse is shifting weight onto his haunches well, we are ready to try a couple of strides in counter-canter. I typically practice the first attempts at counter-canter while riding a big, three-loop serpentine through the whole arena. In doing so, I ride the middle loop very flat and don't worry about reaching the track; this way, the time spent in counter-canter remains short.

At first, it's important to repeat the aids for canter with every stride, if necessary, so the horse doesn't change leads. Once this is working consistently, I can ride a change of direction across half the arena (say from F – E as in the diagram). As I do so, if the horse gets crooked with his hindquarters coming far to the outside and he's not really bearing weight, then he is not moving with straightness and is not on a single track. So, I need to bring the forehand in line with the hindquarters. If the horse changes lead or breaks, I calmly begin again. If the exercise is successful, I decide based on the situation whether to continue the serpentine to completion, or turn onto the track and remain in counter-canter. Before I reach the corner, I transition down to the trot and praise the horse.

*Three-loop serpentine through the whole arena at canter.*

# Flying Changes

Before the rider attempts flying changes, she needs to make sure that the canter is sufficiently collected and that simple changes and counter-canter are both working well. This is when I introduce flying changes. In the beginning, it's typical for the horse to experience some tension as he executes them. From the beginning on, you need to make sure that the horse is straight and coming through from behind. "Coming through" means that the free moment of suspension takes place at the same time with the forehand and hindquarters. Often, especially when the horse is not lowering his hindquarters sufficiently at the canter, he changes lead in front first and then changes behind, that is, he changes late behind. In this case, I initially need to work more on collection (see p. 77), before I practice flying changes again.

Preferably, I begin to introduce flying changes as follows: On a circle at A or C, I begin a figure eight, and as such I repeatedly execute a simple change of lead as I cross the centerline. I like to ride this heading toward the mirrors, so I can see if the horse is really straight with his forehand and hindquarters on a definite single line.

Generally, I lessen the number of walk strides until I do the simple change with just one walk stride remaining. The horse must be cantering with collection and responding to very light aids as he resumes the canter. Ideally, when he himself wants to initiate the canter in the new direction, I then eliminate the walk stride and give the aids for the flying change. As I do so, I shift my weight onto my new inside seat bone, bring my inside leg forward, outside leg back, and give with the inside hand; all of this has the effect of animating the new inside hind to come through more.

*Riding without stirrups, I can easily use the inside of my lower leg to give the aids for the flying change.*

When the change takes place, I always immediately transition to the walk and praise the horse. It is advisable to have a person helping on the ground who can clearly call out "through" or "late," in order for me to be able to give my praise as promptly as possible. If the flying change wasn't good, then I simply ride farther and try again once the horse is responding well to my half-halts.

With some horses, the following has been successful: The rider initially rides several simple changes on the circle, consistently changing to the counter-canter as she approaches the open side and back to the true canter as she approaches the closed side. In doing so, the changes should really take place with just a single walk stride. The rider consistently uses the same location for the changes, which makes it easier for the horse to understand the task. After several simple changes, I just take out the walk stride and try a flying change from counter-canter into true canter. Here, I really need to drive the hindquarters, pick the horse up, and change.

When working on flying changes, it's sometimes advisable not to ride them too often in succession, because particularly the more nervous horses tend to get hot about doing them and become more and more hectic. In this case, it's better to work on something else to distract the horse and then try the change again in another location. With horses that react very sensitively to pressure on their flanks, it can help to ride without spurs so that you can better apply your lower leg. With sensitive horses who like to anticipate the aids, it is important to give clear aids

*A lovely, uphill, "springy" flying change.*

*The horse is straight and coming through well in the flying change.*

and, above all, at the right moment. The timing must be accurate. I like to ride flying changes without stirrups, as I can get even closer with my calf against the horse, and drive more effectively with my seat.

When the horse gets tense after the change, you can counter this either by lengthening the stride on the long side, or transitioning to the walk and praising your horse.

Another good possibility is to introduce the flying change from the half-pass. In half-pass, my horse is already well-collected and cantering uphill. I initially ride out of the corner and begin a half-pass at canter toward the quarterline, hardly positioning the horse at all. When I reach the quarterline, I transition to walk, then pick up the counter-canter. Before the corner, I again ride a simple change to true canter.

When my horse is securely on the aids, carrying himself well and concentrating on working with me, then I practice the same thing again. I begin again with just one walk stride and later without the walk. When I reach the quarterline, I ride a canter stride straight ahead and position my horse in the new direction. Then come the aids for the change. While he's learning, I need to give my aids more definitively, but later, I can slowly allow them to become invisible.

A flying change can only be as good as the quality of the collected canter before the change. The horse should not initiate the change, but rather wait for the rider's aids. Therefore, as the rider, I always need to create new situations. The horse should be moving well uphill, in front of the driving aids, always in a very even rhythm and cantering with collection. In between the changes, I must always canter big and forward, really establishing the impulsion. The goal should be to master the following exercise without errors: I change direction across the short diagonal and ride a flying change as I cross the centerline. I do the same in the other direction, again riding a relaxed flying change as I cross the centerline.

When the flying change is successful, it's exactly the right time to end the training, not allowing the opportunity for further mistakes. I use the good ending then practice again either the next day or the day after that. An abundant chewing of the reins from the hands at the canter is especially important after this work. Then, I transition down to the trot and remain at posting trot as I allow the horse to chew the reins from my hand all the way to the buckle. Here, too, I think about diligent forward movement. Finally, I transition down to the walk. If the work has done my horse good, I'll know it by the satisfied look on his face. And as always, don't forget — praise the horse abundantly.

## Introducing the Double Bridle

When the horse is about six years old, it is about time to get him used to the double bridle. During the first few training sessions when you are riding a young horse with the double bridle, it is recommended that you ride the warm-up in the snaffle bridle so the horse is not already irritated during this phase. During the walk break, the bridles can be switched out. Right from the beginning, it's important that the so-called bridon (snaffle) rein is clearly predominant and the curb bit is used only very lightly, if at all. Dressage horses must become accustomed to the curb as it is required in dressage tests beginning at Third Level.

Even though I personally much prefer to ride with the snaffle bit and do so the majority of the time, I plan a set Double Bridle Day, even in the off-season, during which I do my whole schooling program in the double bridle. When getting horses used to the curb, one problem that can occur is that they just will not seek connection with the unfamiliar bit, at first. They become too light in the hand and I have the feeling they'd like to spit the bit out. You must experiment to find which curb bit the horse will best seek contact with. There are so many differently shaped bits out there: more tongue room or less, long or short shanks, thick or thin bars — you must really rely on experience and test them out individually in order to make a determination as to which feels best to the horse.

*The snaffle rein always predominates.*

*Even wearing her double bridle, Geraldine trots with relaxation through the puddles, stretching long and low.*

## Work In Hand

Once a week, Wilfried Gehrmann provides support for me and my horses with collected work, which takes on additional importance for the horse around age five or six. Mr. Gehrmann, an expert in everything to do with the double longe line and work on long-lines, also guides me from the ground. No matter what level is being ridden, it is important a rider is observed frequently by an experienced teacher, and allows herself to be corrected. From the experienced trainer Wilfried Gehrmann, my horses learn to accept the unfamiliar feel of the long-lines on their hindquarters and to willingly respond to the aids.

Exercises in the highest collection, piaffe, and passage are first required in the upper levels of competition; the introduction of these exercises through the half-step greatly promote muscular development so that carrying power and springiness are developed. The horse's movement becomes more elevated, expressive, and, at the extended gaits, more ground-covering.

Starting to piaffe or passage in short working segments, Wilfried Gehrmann makes sure that the horse maintains rhythm; he corrects irregularities by moving forward. Some horses first offer piaffe, others passage. Based on what the horse finds easier in the beginning, we decide what to work on first with that individual. Frequent and

*Once a week, Wilfried Gehrmann works the horses on the ground.*

abundant praise forms an important building block, with which I can win the horse's trust. If the horse understands the initial approaches to piaffe and passage, I can try it out from the saddle and Mr. Gehrmann works along with me from the ground. As we do this, I initially remain passive, so that in the beginning, the horse is learning to remain balanced with my weight. We use lots of praise to make it clear to him when he responds correctly, and he stays happy and calm. In short working segments, I utilize Mr. Gehrmann's support to improve the carrying power of my horse whose hind legs should lively step up up under his center of gravity. This carrying power is vital in order for him to be able to maintain balance and rhythm when working at the highest levels of collection. As a next step, I take over more and more of the aids until — with ever-decreasing help from the ground — I am able to independently ride the horse in high collection.

As the horse exerts himself more physically and engages his body, it is always important to remain aware that he doesn't get tense. Relaxation with suppleness must remain. When the horse carries his tail with a relaxed swing, it's a sure sign things are going in the right direction. In addition, after this work is complete, it is, of course, time to include forward riding that is full of impulsion. With big, expressive strides, the horse can show that the collected work has yielded positive effects. Allowing him to chew the reins from the hand is especially important in order to stretch the horse completely; equally important is a relaxing walk at the end, which I'll talk about next.

# The Cool-Down Phase

*A secret of successful horse training lies in the art of knowing the right moment to stop. All training sessions should end on a good note and with a positive feeling for horse and rider.*

Only if the horse is in a good state of mind and body when his training comes to an end, will he be motivated by the work when the next day comes around. Still at trot or canter, the horse should slowly chew the reins from the rider's hands, without losing momentum as he does so. The rider should post the trot or be in a light seat at canter. During work, the metabolic processes in the horse's body are heightened and they remain so for 10 – 15 minutes after the hard work has ended. Muscles require far more oxygen and nourishment, and the toxins that have accumulated in the muscles also need to be removed from the system. Until this process is complete, the horse has elevated breathing and heartbeat.

Relaxed trotting while stretching long and low helps to slowly lower respiration, blood pressure, and pulse back to their normal levels. Also, the horse can mentally relax after the work phase. By the end of the training session, he should go, calm and relaxed, at the walk on a loose rein. We like to complete this phase with a short walk outside the ring, either around a pasture or the racetrack. And one thing should never be forgotten: praise the horse for his good collaboration.

*A good ending: walking along...*

*...and munching on the grass.*

# Cavalletti Training

*Cavalletti is a set component of my training program, which is geared toward versatility. I find cavalletti training important and meaningful for every discipline, and every horse at every age.*

My father always used cavalletti regularly when training his horses. Four cavalletti always stood in the riding arena so that he could use them anytime. Today, my horses also benefit from cavalletti training, which I regularly build into the gymnastic training of all of my horses. Even in winter, it's a great way to maintain my event horses' condition and agility and to build up my dressage horses' strength.

## Longeing over Cavalletti

In order to offer my horses lots of variety in their training, they are longed at least once a week. Even more valuable than regular longeing is work on the longe line over cavalletti wearing sliding side-reins, which can guide the horse to go deeper.

For example, training on the longe line over cavalletti is especially valuable for schooling optimal suppleness and coordination. When trotting over cavalletti, the horse should go forward quietly but diligently, and his neck should lower. This means the back is relaxed, the trot full of impulsion, the rhythm even, and the horse trots up well under his center

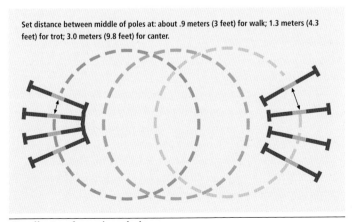

Set distance between middle of poles at: about .9 meters (3 feet) for walk; 1.3 meters (4.3 feet) for trot; 3.0 meters (9.8 feet) for canter.

*Cavalletti set for work on the longe.*

*Loose at the trot and striking off actively, especially with the hind legs.*

of gravity with definite lifting of the legs over the cavalletti. The circle should change often, so that the horse also stays securely on the aids while being longed.

The transitions are the best indicator for how well the horse has remained on the aids. While on the longe, the horse must respond with precision to the aids for both upward and downward transitions. He should be calm and focused at this work. Here, too, it is important the horse is gymnasticized evenly in both directions, so he becomes equally supple on both sides. Above all, effective training over cavalletti on the longe loosens the back. The horse is freed up in his movement, not carrying the rider's weight. During this work, he has to actively think for himself. He must respond to the influence of the hand of the person doing the longeing and the driving aids (using an appropriately long longe whip is important).

When I see how cleverly and skillfully my horse negotiates cavalletti on the longe line, it provides insight into his character, which has interesting implications for his training. It's interesting to see whether he often hits the poles or dislikes coming into contact with them, showing his level of sensitivity. Working from the ground, the person longeing sees interesting details: longe-line training presents the opportunity to observe the horse's facial expression, how he carries his tail, the breathing patterns at the nostril, the activity of the ears, and the way all the muscles work together at all three gaits (these perspectives are more difficult to achieve from the saddle). Sometimes, I become aware of certain anomalies while longeing, which I can then work through and resolve with targeted work under saddle.

## Riding over Cavalletti

Cavalletti work has a physical element: strengthening the muscles while promoting cadence, increased expression and more reliable rhythm. It also has a mental element: cavalletti work requires the horse to think actively and to choose from his own accord to cooperate with his rider. Through this, I also manage to increase his motivation.

Likewise, as the rider, I learn to concentrate as I must choose the right tempo and the right path through the cavalletti. Simultaneously, I need to have my horse securely on my aids.

It's important the distance between cavalletti has been correctly measured, so the horse has a chance of completing the task successfully. The distance between the poles should be .8 – .9 meters (approximately 3 feet) for walk; 1.2 – 1.4 meters (approximately 4 feet) for trot; and about 3 meters (approximately 10 feet) for canter.

*Relaxed strides over cavalletti, incorporating a full stride in between.*

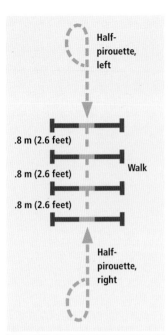

.8 m (2.6 feet)

.8 m (2.6 feet)  Walk

.8 m (2.6 feet)

Half-pirouette, left

Half-pirouette, right

*Half-pirouette at walk, collected walk over cavalletti, half-pirouette at walk.*

## CAVALLETTI ON STRAIGHT LINES

Even with young horses, I begin cavalletti work at the walk on a straight line, following a lead horse. Initially, I ride over a single cavalletti, then two, three, and finally over four. Riding over cavalletti on straight lines develops a ground-covering, diligent, and very rhythmical walk. Here, it's a good idea to allow a full walk stride between two sets of cavalletti. With this arrangement, the horse can rebalance a bit after the first two cavalletti before he needs to step over the next two. This exercise is also useful when multiple horses with different lengths of stride are working together: I use the middle space to add momentum for one horse, while for another, the tempo can be reduced.

On a loose rein, I ride over four walk cavalletti during the initial 10 minute stretching phase, and then again in the walk break between the warm-up phase and the work phase. In the work phase, I ride over the four walk cavalletti on the longest possible rein. I can apply them very well for work on trot-walk transitions, which means I ride at the trot until I'm almost at the cavalletti, then after riding a transition with great feel down to the walk, I ride over the cavalletti.

An advanced exercise is riding at a collected walk over the cavalletti with a half-pirouette at walk, then back over the cavalletti.

## CAVALLETTI ON BENDING LINES

After the horse becomes familiar with straight lines, cavalletti work on a circle at trot or canter is especially valuable, as the horse can be better gymnasticized on a bending line. Above all, exercises on bending lines are good for suppling the horse's inner ribs, and help with

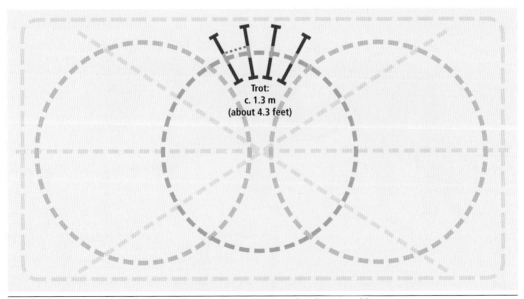

Trot:
c. 1.3 m
(about 4.3 feet)

*Set for trot on the middle circle. All ring figures can be incorporated without a problem.*

*The horse's entire musculature is addressed.*

longitudinal bend and tracking up with the inside hind. Cavalletti training is especially useful for horses that need to step up higher and more diligently with their hind legs.

During warm-up, I trot over the cavalletti on bending lines, allowing the horse to chew the reins from my hands as I do so. In the work phase, I ride at a sitting trot over the cavalletti and, for example, include a trot-walk transition on the side of the circle opposite the cavalletti.

I can also practice trot-canter transitions really well on the bending lines: I ride at trot over the cavalletti, then ride halfway around the circle at canter and just before the cavalletti, I transition down to trot again.

An effective exercise for more advanced horses and riders is the figure-eight on a circle at the trot (see diagram on the next page). Just twice over four cavalletti on the circle works wonders for the suppleness, improvement of flexion and bend, the straightness and throughness of the horse. The rider trots on two voltes of the same size, changing direction after each volte. Through the cones, I ride a horse-length straight ahead and reposition my horse as I do so. The goal is for both half-circles to be ridden exactly the same size and for the horse to

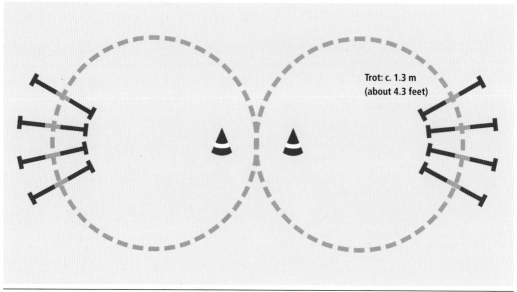

Trot: c. 1.3 m
(about 4.3 feet)

*Figure eight on the circle with two evenly-sized 10-meter voltes.*

demonstrate equally good flexion and bending in both directions.

With every change of direction, the new inside leg comes clearly into contact and drives the horse onto the new outside rein. With some horses, you must really pay attention to giving with the inside hand each time, so the horse doesn't tense up in the neck. If several rounds are successful, you can do this at sitting trot, though of course this exercise should not go on and on endlessly. In between, you should ride the whole arena again, using the long side to increase impulsion, preferably at the posting trot. Afterward, riding lateral movements should be considerably easier for both you and your horse.

### CANTER CAVALLETTI

There are also many interesting exercises for canter work. You can easily imagine that cavalletti training at canter is very demanding. Therefore, short work segments with breaks are important to avoid overwhelming the horse. Canter cavalletti on the circle are excellent for gymnasticizing, especially the inside hind, the back, and the rib cage, as well as for developing longitudinal bend. In the stretching phase, I canter over them in a light seat with the horse travelling long and low; in the work phase, I sit as I canter the circle.

### TROT-CANTER CAVALLETTI

For another exercise that requires a lot of the horse, I position four trot cavalletti on one side of a circle and four canter cavalletti on the opposite side (see diagram). I use cones to mark the point for the transitions. For this exercise, both horse and rider really need to already be "pros" at regular cavalletti work.

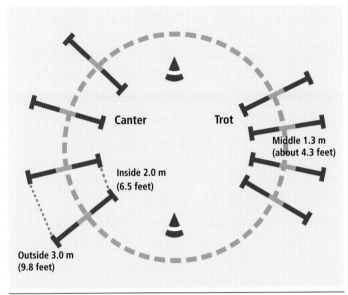

Set up for cavalletti work in trot and canter on a circle.

I canter over the canter cavalletti, transition down to the trot pre-cisely at the cone, and ride over the trot cavalletti. Then, I canter with precision to the next cone. With an experienced horse, I can sit quietly through this sequence as the horse's back muscles are sufficiently strong. Of course, this must be schooled in both directions. It's always important to ride proactively. You must always be looking ahead to the next cone or cavalletti. This exercise speaks to all the valuable ele-ments of cavalletti work and trains the horse's entire musculature. The transitions reinforce throughness with willing cooperation and pre-cise transitions at a distinct point. Maintaining longitudinal bend and going over the eight cavalletti on the circle are real strength-builders.

For those interested in engaging cavalletti work more intensively, I recommend my book (written with my father), *Cavalletti: For Dressage and Jumping.*

## THE ADVANTAGES OF CAVALLETTI WORK FOR THE HORSE

- Improves rhythm and balance in movement
- Gymnasticizes
- Strengthens the musculature
- Loosens the muscles (especially over the back)
- Improves long and low stretch
- Increases suppleness
- Improves surefootedness
- Conditions
- Increases expressiveness in the gaits
- Encourages cadence
- Builds concentration
- Improves motivation through independent thought

# Gymnastic Jumping

*All my horses, including the dressage horses, are regularly ridden over cavalletti, small individual jumps or gymnastic rows. This provides variety. It encourages horses to think actively and independently, while promoting suppleness, coordination, and muscular development.*

Once a week, jumping is part of our training program. Regular gymnastic jumping loosens and strengthens the muscles of the back and hindquarters. This also benefits dressage horses. Riding in a jumping saddle, we either ride through cavalletti exercises at a canter, a gymnastic row, over individual jumps with elements of a stadium course, or with the event horses we may go over small obstacles on the jump course. We begin with gymnasticizing jumping exercises using cavalletti. I'd like to introduce you to three of my favorite exercises.

## Cavalletti on Straight Lines

In this exercise, I set two cavalletti at their highest and placed them 19 meters (62 feet) part. On average, the length of a horse's canter stride ranges from 3 – 3.5 meters (10 – 11.5 feet). You also figure in a canter stride for the take-off and landing phase. So, if the horse canters at a normal tempo over the first cavalletti, he must follow with five canter strides then jump the second cavalletti. The goal of this exercise is to get a feel for the length of each individual canter stride through even, rhythmic cantering. I count along with the canter strides and, initially, ride five strides in between the cavalletti, then I increase the tempo and ride four strides. To finish the exercise, I shorten the canter strides and ride six strides in the distance between the two cavalletti. Varying the canter strides also improves my horse's rideability.

## Jumping on a Circle

With so-called "circle-jumping," four cavalletti set at their highest are placed on a circle (see diagram). To begin, you canter over just two of the cavalletti placed opposite one another, per each round of the

*Looking toward the center of the cavalletti.*

circle; do this before jumping over all four in succession. It can take several rounds of the circle before rider and horse find the appropriate rhythm. Of course, this exercise also needs to be ridden in both directions. The canter strides must always stay even. The rider must always look to the next cavalletti and turn. The inside stirrup turns out and the inside leg drives at the girth.

Another exercise is to choose the outer track, and ride four canter strides instead of three in between the cavalletti. You have mastered this exercise when you can ride a round, alternating between three and four canter strides between the cavalletti, so: 1-2-3, 1-2-3-4, 1-2-3, 1-2-3-4. It's important here, as so often is in life, to quit while you're ahead: this means riding out of the circle early enough, after two or three good rounds.

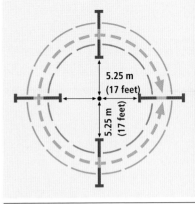

*Jumping on a circle: Four cavalletti evenly spaced on the line of a circle. Ride three canter strides between cavalletti on the inside line; four on the outside.*

## The Cross

The Cross is an advanced exercise. For this, I place four cavalletti like a cross. I now have many options for approaching the cavalletti. The overriding goal is to practice turns. I begin with just two cavalletti and ride a figure eight over both elements. In the beginning, the figure eight consists of two 10-meter voltes; later, I can ride ever-smaller turns, which ridden in collected canter almost resemble a quarter-pirouette. After these turns are working well in both directions, I can jump over the middle of the cross, practicing an exact approach over the narrow center.

*The Cross lends itself well to practicing turns.*

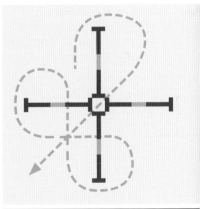

*These are just two of the possibilities for jumping over the cross.*

*01 The horse trots over the cavalletti...*

*02 ...jumps over the cross-rail...*

## 👉 SAMPLE GYMNASTIC

**Gymnastic rows are built with one obstacle after another. How often each exercise is repeated depends entirely on how securely and fluidly the horse has completed it. When the horse is rushing over the trot cavalletti, you should approach the row from a turn. When he's sluggish, ride forward up the preceding long side in a diligent tempo, and carry this impulsion through the turn.**

For young horses, I would include a maximum of four jumps in a gymnastic row, with their height ranging from about .8 – 1 meter (2.5 – 3 feet). This is just one sample exercise from my practice. The possible variations are endless.

Through the firing of the muscles of the hindquarters, muscle development is boosted. The all-important stretch with long neck and lifted back (bascule), vital to jumping technique, is substantially furthered. Above all, horses really take pleasure in jumping.

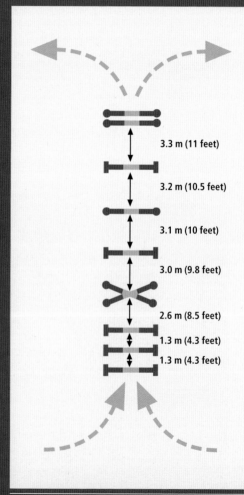

3.3 m (11 feet)

3.2 m (10.5 feet)

3.1 m (10 feet)

3.0 m (9.8 feet)

2.6 m (8.5 feet)

1.3 m (4.3 feet)

1.3 m (4.3 feet)

*Example of gymnastic grid.*

*03 ...lands and looks to the cavalletti...*

*04 ...canters over the cavalletti...*

*05 ...jumps over the vertical...*

*06 ...lands...*

*07 ...canters over the cavalletti...*

*08 ...and jumps the oxer.*

# Narrow Jumps

## ... Step by Step

01

02

*Always introduce your horse to narrow jumps very gradually.*

Today, jumping over narrow jumps and corners belong among the standard requests made at every three-day event. It requires much practice and trust between horse and rider. To introduce the horse to these jumps, you can add guide poles as wings for the side of narrow jumps, and also a ground pole directly before the obstacle as a guide for take-off. By and by, the exercise can be made more difficult by laying the side poles on the ground. As a final step, the guide poles can be removed altogether.

For those who want to work intensively on jumping, I recommend my book *Cavalletti: For Dressage and Jumping* as well as *Basic Training of the Young Horse*. There, you'll find important fundamental knowledge explained in detail as well as abundant diagrams of jumping exercises.

03    04

01 Narrow jump with winged standards.

02 Narrow jump with wings and water mat.

03 Narrow jump with guide poles added.

04 A harder request: Narrow jump without poles or standards.

05 Getting a bit narrower still.

06 Goal met: it doesn't get any narrower.

05    06

# Training on Hills

*Training on hills is part of our regular working program — for dressage horses, also. Going uphill and working on hills strengthens the entire musculature, promotes conditioning, and is good for the horse's balance and surefootedness.*

Ideally, we travel to hills for training every fifth day. There, we begin with a 10 – 15 minute stretching phase at the walk — good training for building up the horse's entire musculature. When we begin uphill, the horse must strike off very energetically from behind and use his whole back. In the beginning, I must make sure not to ride up- or downhill when it's too steep: a horse needs to adjust slowly to the new demand being made of him. With regular training, the overall steepness can be increased.

*Galloping uphill, calmly and harmoniously.*

*Hill work promotes balance...*

*...and coordination.*

At the end of the stretching phase at the walk, I work in posting trot at an easy tempo for 10 – 15 minutes. In trot, I also work both uphill and downhill. Training on the hills is especially exciting for stallions as it presents many new sensations for them to process. Temporarily, this excitement promotes a dynamic through which you can enhance the horse's entire way of going, making it more expressive, imposing, and cadenced. When riding uphill, you bend slightly forward and push your weight down into your heels. Of course, the horse must, at some point, learn to trot downhill and maintain his balance as he does so. As this takes place, you bring your upper body back slightly, in order to always keep your seat in balance with the horse.

## Training at Canter/Gallop

After the trot phase, I canter on at a quiet tempo. Often, with young horses, the canter work on hills is often still weak. Most of the time, horses that are familiar with this exercise accelerate as the hill gets steeper. On the other hand, young horses often lose power quickly and, for example, break to trot. Initially, allow your horse to go in his chosen tempo and do not drive him uphill. You should always introduce this training to a young horse very slowly and carefully, so as not to overwhelm him. While the horse may have become accustomed to varying ground conditions while going uphill, coming downhill really

*Bobby and Escada sprint with lots of enthusiasm.*

requires the highest levels of concentration.

When cantering in a large group, it's a given that there is the danger of horses egging each other on and getting hot. Therefore, it's advisable to work in small groups. Only horses that fit together well based on their level of training should get to canter together. But it is not only the horse's training level that needs to be considered: what's inside is also a decisive factor. For example, ambitious Bobby always wants to try to pass the equally ambitious Escada. Therefore, at a certain point in their conditioning, they must go their separate ways, otherwise, they simply gallop much too fast. In contrast, the amiable Soma will happily canter more calmly with Geraldine, and they can easily take turns following one another when ridden. Along these lines, Weisse Düne is easy to regulate, even when she is following other horses (although, this may change with time).

The more regularly and often the horses gallop in the hills, the more conditioned and strong they become. This can definitely increase their motivation and ambition, and then the groups need to be reorganized to accommodate. Therefore, begin gallop work very quietly, not galloping for more than 2 minutes. If your horse still has enough strength, you can take a 3-minute walk break and then gallop uphill again one more time. Afterward, slowly transition down to a trot, spending 5 – 10 minutes at a slow trot before finally transitioning to the walk. We ride long enough at the walk for the pulse and breath of our horses to completely return to normal.

# Interval Training

With my event horses, I complete an interval training once every five days in order to target conditioning and performance ability for cross-country. I find the five-day time span optimal: the body has been stimulated by the training and must preserve its effects for this length of time in order to meet the increasing demands. The recovery phase is then long enough and on the days in between, the horse can be worked normally. The day after gallop training is a recovery day. Either the horse has it off completely or he is just stretched out or longed.

For interval training, we also begin with 15 minutes at the walk, then 10 – 15 minutes of posting trot. In the first gallop phase, I begin with an easy tempo then slowly increase. Sprints come into play only at the end of the training plan. As Chris Bartle once told me, "speed kills." Therefore, I ride only short faster stages, increasing the horse's training before a long test.

Interval training ends by calmly cantering out, trotting out, and abundant walking.

---

**INTERVAL TRAINING**

I generally divide interval training as follows: three gallop intervals with 3-minute walk or trot breaks in between. The length and distance of the individual gallop intervals depends on the available training opportunities. Both the speed and the degree of steepness influence the heart rate. The number of repetitions and the pauses in between, the time (2 – 3 minutes), the tempo (trot or walk), are just as much parameters as is the condition of the footing. Endurance, power, and speed build condition. After initially training for endurance, strength training comes next, and finally speed.

---

# *Hacking Out*

*"Going for a romp," as my father always referred to when riding out in the open, is a fixed component of the versatile and diversified training plan I use for my horses. Riding in nature is not only fun, but also schools the horses in a variety of ways.*

## Strict Rules

When riding out in the open, we always ride together in a group. On the weekends, when we are not competing, there are often as many as 12 horses hacking out together on our beloved Sunday rides. It resembles a company outing with family, the team, and friends. The joy of riding in nature always remains at the forefront, but in order to be able

*Every ride out in the open also begins with a long walk.*

*Side-by-side in pairs at a calm trot.*

to enjoy the outing, we abide by some strict rules. It's helpful for young horses to be able to orient themselves around more experienced horses, who serve as brave and secure leaders. We follow one another in a group, always with two horses abreast. The stallions are ridden at a safe distance from the mares. The riding order is always suited to the horses' temperaments, and we also ensure that a safe distance of two to three horse lengths is always maintained. We know exactly who likes to go with whom and what everyone's "quirks" are. Bobby will kick out high — and also purposefully — when someone dares to try to pass him. By and by, the horses learn both to change places and to adjust themselves to a new spot.

On a first trail ride with a young horse, only walk and trot should be attempted; the canter can be added once the horse is secure and easily controlled. The most important ground rule: when riding toward home, we do not increase the speed. And, at the end of the ride, we walk.

# Getting Used to Environmental Stimuli

Getting used to environmental stimuli is important and necessary for every horse. It strengthens their courage and promotes relaxation in new and unfamiliar situations. I find this especially valuable when my horses and I attend competitions and they have to leave their familiar environment.

In order to gradually get young horses used to different environmental stimuli, we always choose the least exciting possible route for our first time out. Once the horses are further along in their training and are responding well to their riders' aids, I can trust them on new

*Ridden over hilly terrain, the horse really learns to balance himself well.*

trails and get them used to more unfamiliar situations, such as clattering farm equipment, tractors passing by, and so on. Along with us, there is a relaxed horse who, unafraid and confident, leads everyone past. This is an important support system for the less experienced horses. But, it is also my task as the rider to convey confidence to my horse. Hacking out in the open lends itself perfectly to enhancing a trusting relationship with a horse and becoming a team. It's especially important that my event horses don't become distracted by environmental stimuli so we can rely upon one another on a demanding cross-country course.

## Surefootedness

Hacking trains the horse's entire body. It's important to me that my horse can move on different types of footing. Riding out in the open develops dexterity and surefootedness and is an optimal way to get the horse used to different types of footing. As weather conditions allow, every type of groundcover can be great for this: for example, grass, sand, or the forest floor whether going uphill or downhill.

When training event horses, it is even customary to travel on harder surfaces for extended periods at the walk or shorter periods at the trot, in order to strengthen the tendons and ligaments. Of course, a prerequisite for this is that the horses are well-shod.

# Getting Accustomed to Water

I take my time to carefully get all my horses accustomed to water. This level of comfort is important for all my horses, no matter what discipline they specialize in: my dressage horses should not let a puddle in the corner interfere with their work, just as my showjumpers or event horses must bravely jump into water and gallop through it.

Therefore, I try as much as possible to plan to visit different water sites when we're out on the trails. From the first contact onward, it's important to make sure the water is not too deep, the entry point is not too steep, and the footing conditions are not too difficult. When ridden in a group and following a confident lead horse, it becomes much easier for most young horses to take that first step. In the water, it is still important to keep a conscious and safe distance from the other horses.

After a while, you'll see that horses really come to enjoy the water to the fullest, whether having a drink or simply splashing around in the cool wetness. As a rider, it's always a true pleasure for me to experience this.

*Franz canters through water as a matter of course.*

*A joyful outing: We always hack out in a group.*

# My Horses
## — Character Types from Shy to Go-Getter

# *Escada*
## — The World-Class Horse

With Escada, I immediately start gushing. She's an extremely special mare with much charisma and supreme confidence. Her ability cross-country and in stadium is boundless; her courage and willingness to perform, beyond compare. She is a dominant lead mare who knows exactly what she likes and what she doesn't. Now and then, she can really demonstrate it. Generally, Escada is very sensitive and refined. During groundwork, she responds to the tiniest aids and when I ride her with a neck ring and without a saddle, she is very attentive.

Escada came to my barn shortly after she turned eight. She had received good fundamental training from Andreas Brand and, from the start, she was a very trusting and capable jumper. She had exceptionally elastic, supple gaits, full of impulsion. Thanks to the lively strike-off from her hind feet, her trot has cadence and is very expressive. "This horse just doesn't have any weaknesses," I thought, as I rode

*Galloping uphill.*

**SAP ESCADA FRH**

| | |
|---|---|
| **Nickname:** | Mousey |
| **Breed:** | Hanoverian mare by Embassy/out of Lehnsherr |
| **Breeder:** | Johanna Stuhtmann |
| **Owner:** | Madeleine Winter-Schulze, DOKR, Ingrid Klimke, Hanoverian Association |
| **Born:** | 2004 |
| **Character:** | Sensitive, refined, intelligent, bold, fearless, confident, ambitious |
| **What Escada likes:** | Galloping fast, jumping, being petted, relaxing out at pasture |
| **What Escada doesn't like:** | Other mares, to be alone |
| **Discipline:** | Eventing |
| **Level of Training:** | Completely trained to the Four-Star level |

her that first week. She shone with her elastic movement, played with the challenges on both stadium and cross-country courses, and was overall very refined and brave.

Then, I rode my first three-day event with her, and realized with surprise I was sitting on a firecracker. I had to keep my full concentration just to steer her through the test, but in fact, I was just a passenger and Escada just kept getting "hotter." So, I did actually have the task of relaxing with her and, to be honest, it was not easy in the beginning. At first, it was hard to imagine her relaxing in a dressage test. It took time before she concentrated, showed obedience to the exercise, and really paid attention to me. In our first winter together, I practiced lots of dressage with her and in the beginning of the season, I only entered her in dressage competitions. Gaining experience did her good.

Even today, I often take her with me to competitions even if she herself is not competing. I then ride her there in the warm-up ring and practice a dressage test in the arena. When I travel to a dressage show, it's a good training opportunity to ride Escada in lots of different dressage arenas. In this way, she learns to concentrate in an unfamiliar environment and to relax. Even today, Escada can still anticipate a test component. She is simply very smart and knows exactly which movements come in which order in a dressage test.

*SAP Escada FRH is a beautiful mare; a model rectangular build.*

*Champion at the 2015 Three-Star event in Aachen.*

Escada is absolutely the best horse I have had under saddle to date. In the beginning, I often thought to myself "just don't ruin this wonderful horse" and was actually a bit awe-struck by her immense quality. With her, I cannot allow myself to forget to ride well, even though she is without doubt a world-class horse.

It was a high point when we won the 2015 Four-Star event in Luhmühlen. There, she really demonstrated her class. It's a joy to work with her each day. It is my job to keep her fit, motivated, and focused. We pay attention to providing training rich in variety with lots of playful moments. During the competitive season, we often gallop in the hills to build up her condition. At the team trainings, we work on technical cross-country elements or practice dressage tests. At home, either Carmen or I will happily ride Escada without a saddle and with just a neck ring. She enjoys it as much as we do, and she is very sensitive when we ride her this way. I believe, once you have won over a lead mare, she will go through fire for you.

## Escada's Training Plan

Escada's workload consists of galloping in hills for conditioning training (interval training every fifth day during the season), dressage, cavalletti work (also on the longe), and enjoyable hacking out in the open. It's rare that I complete a show-jumping competition or train cross-country with her. Gymnastic jumping is part of her regular plan.

**SAMPLE WEEKLY TRAINING PLAN**

**Monday:**
Free day, out to pasture

**Tuesday:**
Dressage-oriented cavalletti work

**Wednesday:**
Ride dressage exercises and a test

**Thursday:**
Jumping with cavalletti, gymnastic jumping

**Friday:**
Dressage, ride a test

**Saturday:**
Longeing over cavalletti

**Sunday:**
Hill work or hacking

# *Hale Bob*
## — The Determined One

Bobby is a bay Oldenburg gelding who I bought as a five-year old, after a friend of mine discovered him at a show jumping competition. I took special notice of him because, like my earlier event horse Seacookie, Bobby was sired by the stallion Helikon XX. Some of my friends couldn't understand why I even bought this plain bay gelding who, at first glance, seemed kind of average. In the beginning, he looked more like an Irish Cob, with a big head and shorter neck. But I liked Bobby from the start and at that point, my top priority was finding an event horse that had a really good jump. Bobby met these criteria.

Before he came to me, he had already been brought along exclusively as a showjumper and I knew he would surely have some catching up to do in terms of dressage. What I did not know was that he also was quite capable of throwing wild bucks from time to time — always when he's excited, "fresh," and wants to show his zest for life, especially when we're galloping cross-country.

*Bobby doesn't lose any time in jumping.*

**HORSEWARE HALE BOB OLD**

| | |
|---|---|
| **Nickname:** | Bobby |
| **Breed:** | Oldenburg gelding by Helikon XX/out of Noble Champion |
| **Breeder:** | Dr. Rolf Lueck |
| **Owner:** | Ingrid Klimke |
| **Born:** | April 25, 2004 |
| **Character:** | A courageous fighter, calm, and attentive |
| **What Bobby likes:** | His friend Escada, carrots, pasture time, bucking while galloping in the hills or out hacking, swimming |
| **What Bobby doesn't like:** | Apples, civilized cantering in his assigned place when out with a group, standing calmly in the start box |
| **Discipline:** | Eventing |
| **Level of Training:** | Completely trained to the Four-Star level |

*Cavalletti training keeps Bobby supple.*

He was really challenging that first year and I often times had difficulty controlling him cross-country. In the time since, he has put this stormy and stressful phase behind him. However, I must always possess good command of the defensive seat when riding him, especially when he is overcome with joy or initiative.

When handled, Bobby is mostly quiet and relaxed. In the barn or when turned out, he's not quick to get agitated about things. Wearing sliding side-reins and working in the dressage arena, he is even a wonderful school horse for children. However, when the time comes and we're competing or training on the hills, his ears perk up and he is totally ready to go. Bobby knows exactly when things are going to get exciting and he saves his energy for these moments. When he's excited, he can be highly explosive.

Bobby was six years old when he started his first competitive season. He made the national finals and even placed in a CIC*. From then on, he consistently placed well in CIC** events. When he was seven, he completed the season by taking part in the World Championships for Young Eventing Horses in Le Lion d'Angers, France. At eight, he won the Westphalian Championships in Velen, Germany. Because of Bobby, I learned about and came to appreciate African safari on horseback: he won the Indoor Derby at the German Championships in Stuttgart for us, and the prize was a dream vacation at "Wait a Little" in Africa. At nine, Bobby really came into his own, and showed that he could be secure and successful at Three Stars. I completed my first Four Star with Bobby in Pau in 2014. In 2015, we placed second at the Four Star Badminton event and we were part of the gold-medal winning team at the European Championships in Blair Castle, England.

Thanks to the combination of his efficient and economical gallop, his jumping ability, and fighting heart, he is a wonderful event horse.

*Horseware Hale Bob OLD has a rectangular build and good muscling throughout his body.*

*Relaxing after work is done.*

Cross-country, we're always very fast as Bobby does not lose any time at the jumps. He possesses great staying power, which has shown even more so at the long Three and Four Star events.

With Bobby, I find it very valuable to have solid dressage work. With cavalletti training, longeing over cavalletti, and loosening dressage training, we work on his suppleness. Dressage is definitely not Bobby's strength, as he doesn't possess an overly generous quality of movement. He overcomes this in the test with suppleness and obedience. I'm fascinated by how he reacts to my aids with such refinement and sensitivity. This heightens our chances for an error-free dressage test, which positions us well as we go into the cross-country and show-jumping phases.

My father was right, "Good horses are made." Bobby is the best example of this and I am so happy to know him. He's demonstrated a fantastic development and is a true companion who is highly motivated at competitions consistently fighting for me.

## Bobby's Training Plan

Bobby needs lots of gymnasticizing. For him, an extensive stretching phase is especially important. In his dressage training, I place a high value on correct flexion and bend. I ride Bobby on many bending lines, always wanting to foster suppleness through his rib cage above all. Or, we longe over cavalletti — also in order to keep him loose and supple while on the circle. For conditioning, we do interval training in the hills, about once every five days.

**SAMPLE WEEKLY TRAINING PLAN**

**Monday**:
Free day, out to pasture

**Tuesday:**
Dressage-oriented cavalletti work

**Wednesday:**
Extensive loosening under saddle and dressage work

**Thursday:**
Cavalletti work, gymnastic jumping

**Friday:**
Longeing over cavalletti

**Saturday:**
Competition or dressage work

**Sunday:**
Conditioning with hill work

# *Parmenides*
## — Jumping Is His Calling

Parmi came to my barn at the end of his third year so that I could train him from the beginning. A fantastic gallop, courage, carefulness, and jumping ability are his most outstanding qualities. He is in his element when jumping — as much cross-country as in stadium. When jumping, he's very able, attentive, careful, eager, and clever.

Full of energy and always applying himself joyfully when jumping, Parmi imparts his zest for life to me. Dressage was never his strength, as his nerves and the mechanics of his trot make it difficult for him. At five, he was able to win the bronze medal in eventing at the National Championships in Warendorf, as well as secure a spot in the show-jumping finals. By doing so, he became the first horse to successfully take part in the finals of two competitions — eventing and show-jumping — in the history of the National Championships.

In his sixth and seventh years, Parmi gained lots of experiences, in both the CIC* and CIC** area and in show-jumping, where he was

*Brave over the KOSMOS corner.*

---

**PARMENIDES**

| | |
|---|---|
| **Nickname:** | Parmi |
| **Breed:** | Trakehner gelding by Sir Chamberlain/out of Habicht |
| **Breeder:** | Marion Gottschalk |
| **Owner:** | Marion and Eric Gottschalk |
| **Born:** | 2004 |
| **Character:** | Sensitive, high performer, brave |
| **What Parmi likes:** | Jumping, jumping, jumping — and preferably bucking afterward |
| **What Parmi doesn't like:** | Standing still, walking in a civilized manner when being turned out |
| **Discipline:** | Jumping |
| **Level of Training:** | Completely trained to the Three-Star level of eventing and Advanced-Level show-jumping |

*Parmi jumps with good bascule and technique.*

*Parmi always gallops attentively toward the jump with ears pricked forward.*

victorious through Medium Level. The crowning glory: World Championships for Event Horses in Le Lion d'Angers (CCI**).

As an eight-year-old, Parmenides established himself in Three-Star events. He placed at every start. The high point of the season was the World Cup in Malmö. Here, Parmi once again proved he was ready to play at this advanced level. Afterward, we decided to take a break, allowing him to recover from an injury. Parmi went back to his breeder in Hessen while he was convalescing, then returned to our competition barn as a nine-year-old.

Together with his breeders and owners Marion and Eric Gottschalk, we decided to reintroduce him to competition exclusively as a show-jumper. On the show-jumping course, he had shown us over and over again how much he loves to jump. He's already won a One-Star Advanced Level completion in a jump-off and also won the Indoor Event in Stockholm.

For jumping, Parmi is my "good mood" horse. It's clearly his calling. He seeks the jump outright and is very agile and fast on course. For Parmi, it's enough if I let the reins out over the jump and look in the direction I want to go — with that, he knows what to do. He's so motivated during this whole thing that it is not uncommon for him to buck for joy after a jump. Parmi and I are a well-practiced team. He totally has fun when jumping and is very ambitious. If and when he does make a mistake on course, he will take the next jump considerably higher and rounder.

For me, it's a wonderful opportunity to try out new things — whether jumping in costume, obstacle jumping, speed derbies, or indoor three-phase events. No matter what we do, I can always rely on Parmi's fighting spirit. If he does not get to jump regularly at home, he gets bored. When he then sees a jump has appeared in our riding arena, his ears always perk back up immediately.

### SAMPLE WEEKLY TRAINING PLAN

**Monday:** Dressage-oriented gymnastic work over cavalletti

**Tuesday:** Loosening work at canter on the track

**Wednesday:** Cavalletti work, gymnastic jumping

**Thursday:** Longeing over cavalletti

**Friday:** Jumping

**Saturday:** Hacking or competition

**Sunday:** Free day, out to pasture

*Parmenides is a friendly and sensitive Trakehner gelding.*

# *Franziskus*
## — The Go-Getter

Franziskus is a bay Hanovarian stallion who, overall, causes a sensation wherever he goes. He is standing at the stud farm Holkenbrink. Since the end of Franziskus's fifth year, he has been trailered over to me for riding. The Holkenbrink family and team support us. Especially Wilhelm Holkenbrink, who most often transports Franziskus to us, and follows the development of his stallion with enthusiasm.

Franziskus is one impressive figure. For him physically, the sky's the limit, and he possesses an outstanding quality of movement. Above all, the mechanics of his trot are demonstrative of this quality. The focus of his training is often basic obedience, throughness with willing cooperation and solid fundamentals. Franz learns new exercises playfully and with motivation then likes to show off what he's learned.

Franziskus has at his command both good self-confidence and mental strength. He's a typical stallion. As a breeding stallion, he

*Franziskus enjoys jumping.*

**FRANZISKUS**

| | |
|---|---|
| **Nickname:** | Franz |
| **Breed:** | Hanoverian stallion by Fidertanz/out of Alabaster |
| **Breeder:** | E. Albers, Loeningen |
| **Owner:** | Wilhelm Holkenbrink |
| **Born:** | 2008 |
| **Character:** | Confident, headstrong |
| **What Franz likes:** | Extended trot, covering mares, rolling |
| **What Franz doesn't like:** | Loud noises, other stallions and certain geldings |
| **Discipline:** | Dressage |
| **Level of Training:** | At six, took part in National Championships and World Championships for young dressage horses; at seven, champion in dressage at Intermediare I |

sometimes likes to pay attention to other horses, most often rivals and mares. For example, when he's working in the arena with another horse that he doesn't like, I need to really watch out and maintain control.

Because Franziskus can be a very dominant horse, I pay especial attention to the necessary obedience. When he came to me, he first of all had to learn the basic exercise of halting and standing still. In the beginning, he really did not even notice me because he was so focused on his environment. He was very bewildered when all of a sudden someone up above him wanted to set the tone. With Franz, it is very important that he never catches on how strong he really is. Then, I would have lost, as in addition to his physical strength, he is also very strong-willed. He would always try to have his own way. So, I do all I can to motivate him and keep work interesting; for example, I stretch him out on the galloping track, do lots of cavalletti work, or practice dressage work out in a mowed field.

His strength is flying changes. I have never ridden a horse his age that learned flying changes as easily as Franz. He has fun, never gets confused, and moves very much uphill when he does them.

*Franziskus likes flying changes, which he learned playfully and easily.*

*Franziskus: brilliant type and a substantial frame.*

# Franziskus's Training Plan

Even when Franziskus is not staying with us at our barn, we take it upon ourselves to direct his training so that he gets as much variety as possible. His training begins with a stretching phase on our track. Here, he will be loosened up under saddle at all three basic gaits. Like all the other horses, Franziskus is ridden over cavalletti for gymnastic effect. At the trot, I like the cavalletti at the middle height for him, as he naturally has enough cadence and impulsion for this height. Franziskus's athletic future clearly lies in dressage. Training sessions in the double bridle and work in hand on long-lines do him good. He learns new exercises and solidifies what he already knows. In the competition season, I'll begin competing him at Prix. St. Georges in dressage. At home, Sophie Holkenbrink rides him on the days when I cannot. Most important for Franziskus is basic obedience. The longer and more frequently I ride him, the better he knows to attune himself to me. We are growing together as a team.

**SAMPLE WEEKLY TRAINING PLAN**

| | |
|---|---|
| **Monday:** | Foundational work, gymnasticizing dressage exercises with cavalletti |
| **Tuesday:** | Practice new dressage movements |
| **Wednesday:** | A relaxed, suppling ride at home |
| **Thursday:** | Foundational work |
| **Friday:** | Long-lining or work in hand: an emphasis on collection with Mr. Gehrmann |
| **Saturday:** | Ride a test in a double bridle or snaffle |
| **Sunday:** | Franziskus is at home, standing at stud |

# *Geraldine*
## — The Shy One

Today, Geraldine is a large-framed, elegant chestnut mare who shines in the large dressage arena. She grew up with the herd at the Gut Schwaighof, the facility of her breeders and part owners, Hannelore and Ulrich Zeising. They informed me that Geraldine was ranked rather low in the herd as a foal. The Zeisings showed her to me as a three-year-old and we turned her loose to move about in the indoor arena. She had a light, floating trot and I liked her. I could also see that she was going to first need to grow into her large body and definitely needed more time to develop. We decided to send her to my former apprentice, Lara Heggelmann, who thoroughly and carefully

*At the National Championships.*

**GERALDINE**

| | |
|---|---|
| **Nickname:** | Trine |
| **Breed:** | Out of a Rhinelander mare by Fürst Grandios/By Tolstoi |
| **Breeder:** | Ulrich and H. Johanna Zeising "Gut Schwaighof" |
| **Owner:** | Ulrich and Hannelore Zeising "Gut Schwaighof," Faith Berghuis, Ingrid Klimke |
| **Born:** | 2008 |
| **Character:** | Shy, gentle, and sensitive |
| **What Geraldine likes:** | Being petted extensively, a good mash |
| **What Geraldine doesn't like:** | Loud noises (from motors), too many horses, and being too close to other horses when ridden, being in her stall without her neighbors close by |
| **Discipline:** | Dressage |
| **Level of Training:** | At six, took part in National Championships; at seven, placed at Prix St. Georges |

*Geraldine works with focus.*

*Praise increases her sense of security.*

trained her through Second Level. Afterward, Geraldine returned to my barn at the end of her fifth year.

Geraldine is a quiet and reserved horse. She is shy and was often afraid in the beginning, especially when ridden out in front of other horses. In the beginning, she did not trust herself to lead the group when riding out, but she did not feel comfortable in the middle of the group, either. She went at the back of the group and put a big distance between herself and the other horses, which fascinated us at first. She let the distance get bigger and bigger and gave the impression she would prefer having nothing to do with the other horses. Over the years, her behavior has changed: today, she will bravely take the lead and stays with the group, as long as the others don't get too close for her liking. Geraldine is a sound-sensitive horse and whenever anything is new for her, she finds it daunting at first. We have tried to be very cautious when getting her used to new things and to increase her self-confidence. When she does something well, I always praise her and build in a walk break. In this way, she knows everything is all right. She can relax and I win her trust. She is very sensitive to ride, so I really need to concentrate fully on her and give my aids with feel.

Geraldine is very good natured and always very motivated. She wants to do everything right and always tries her best. In the barn, she is also very sociable and well behaved. Just being left alone is not her thing. Without her stablemates, she does not feel at ease.

## Geraldine's Training Plan

In order for Geraldine to learn to relax when being ridden in a group, we always take her with us on our hacks and adventures. I'm of the opinion it will help her to experience being ridden out in the open. Of course, she is also worked on the longe line once a week and ridden over cavalletti for gymnastic benefits. As Geraldine's future lies clearly in dressage, it has also become the emphasis of her training. This means, I do dressage-oriented work with her four days a week. She learns new exercises step by step and I'm currently beginning to compete her at Prix St. Georges. In order for her to be able to learn new exercises well, it's important there is a relaxed atmosphere in the riding arena or the indoor where she's working. Most significantly for Geraldine, we really need to master that which she's already learned, so that she can demonstrate it with self-confidence.

When — and only when — the fundamentals are good, I can go further with her training, step by step. At the moment, Geraldine is secure with all exercises at Prix St. Georges and she has successfully begun learning collected steps, working in the direction of piaffe and passage.

### SAMPLE WEEKLY TRAINING PLAN

| | |
|---|---|
| **Monday:** | Free day, out to pasture |
| **Tuesday:** | Gymnasticizing dressage, incorporating cavalletti |
| **Wednesday:** | Work on a loose rein, work in hand, dressage exercises |
| **Thursday:** | Longeing over cavalletti |
| **Friday:** | Practice new dressage exercises in the double bridle |
| **Saturday:** | Cavalletti work or jumping or hacking out |
| **Sunday:** | Competition or ride a test |

*Hill training for strength and conditioning with Andreas.*

# *Weisse Düne*
## — The Supremely Confident

Weisse Düne is a friendly and well-balanced gray mare who wins over everyone in the barn with her attentive and trusting character. She has a wonderful attitude toward being ridden, loves to learn, and is cooperative, motivated, and consistent at work.

Our national trainer, Hans Melzer, saw the gray mare going cross-country with Marina Köhncke up and recommended her to me. Weisse Düne was bred by Hanno Köhncke. At his facility, she was raised well and enjoyed a solid basic training.

Weisse Düne earned her nickname while on the island of Norderney. On our vacation there with the horses, we got to know her better, and she quickly won over our hearts. So, too, she quickly became good friends with the other horses in the barn. "Biene," which means "bee"

*Weisse Düne at the World Championships for young event horses.*

**WEISSE DÜNE**

| | |
|---|---|
| **Nickname:** | Biene |
| **Breed:** | Out of a Holsteiner mare by Clarimo/By Romino |
| **Breeder:** | Hanno Köhncke |
| **Owner:** | Marion Drache, Ingrid Klimke |
| **Born:** | 2009 |
| **Character:** | Balanced, capable, and supremely confident |
| **What Weisse Düne likes:** | Stomping in water, galloping on the beach, eating |
| **What Weisse Düne doesn't like:** | When she is not the first one fed, changes in her familiar environment (tarps, tractors) |
| **Discipline:** | Eventing |

*A good example of chewing reins from the hand.*

in German, always seems to be content with both herself and her environment. She is very people-oriented and bright.

Biene has good basic gaits and a ground-covering, nimble gallop. She has huge movement and shows her heart when jumping or going cross-country. Weisse Düne is predisposed to be level-headed and intelligent. In these ways, she meets every expectation I wish for in an event horse.

In dressage, she learns new exercises easily, thanks to her enjoyment of work and desire to always get everything right. As a six-year-old, Biene won multiple One Star events, and was fifth in the national championships with my apprentice, Philipp Wessling. At the World Eventing Championships for Young Horses, she showed her whole potential. In the dressage arena, she was focused and

*A joyful buck while training at gallop.*

*Weisse Düne has the good conformation necessary to be a versatile horse.*

strongly expressive, cross-country she galloped and jumped great despite an unlucky refusal, and in show-jumping she put forth a confident, clean round.

Every day, it brings me great joy to ride Weisse Düne. She sometimes perceives things as "dangerous" and wants to spook or doesn't want to go past (e.g. tarps or tractors). Then I need to be consistent and ride her in shoulder-in past the "dangerous" place until she gives up and earns her praise. Ridden bareback and with a neck ring, she is very sensitive and attentive, just as she is during groundwork and when trained on a line.

## Biene's Training Plan

Weisse Düne has been built up step by step. She enjoys variety in her training with cavalletti work, jumping, and conditioning work in the hills. Also in her dressage training, she is being developed as appropriate for her age.

---

**SAMPLE WEEKLY TRAINING PLAN**

| | |
|---|---|
| **Monday:** | Free day, out to pasture |
| **Tuesday:** | Dressage work, new exercises |
| **Wednesday:** | Cavalletti work |
| **Thursday:** | Dressage, also practicing a test |
| **Friday:** | Jumping |
| **Saturday:** | Longeing over cavalletti |
| **Sunday:** | Galloping in the hills, hacking out, or competition |

# *Königssee*
## — The Model Student

Königssee is a very "typey," dark bay Trakehner stallion with a magnificent face. He's not necessarily the biggest guy out there, but he makes himself big. Physically, he has got a harmonious build and is well proportioned. Königssee is a bright horse, who has a buck in him.

After his first season at stud, he came to me for training as a three-year-old. Together with my then-apprentice, Pia Rumpel, he went through his basic training.

Whether he's in the dressage arena, on a show-jumping course, or going cross-country, he is always very sure of himself and confident at work. When jumping, he's brave and very level-headed. It's not only at competitions that he is a true model student: self-motivated and possessing strong nerves, he learns new tasks quickly and is uncomplicated. New experiences or noises don't throw him off. He concentrates fully on his rider and is both very obedient and honest in all jumping and cross-country exercises. With young horses and horses that are still developing their muscles, like Königssee, there will be many breaks in their training when they are turned out to pasture. My goal is to develop the horse, without overextending him.

At home, Königssee is very stallion-like. There, he will frequently allow himself be distracted by nice gray mares or will show off for his

*Good form over the vertical.*

**KÖNIGSSEE**

| | |
|---|---|
| **Breed:** | Trakehner Stallion by Intercontie/out of Tambour |
| **Breeder:** | Dr. Elke Söchtig, Gut Elmarshausen |
| **Owner:** | Marita Schreiber |
| **Born:** | May 13, 2010 |
| **Character:** | Confident, intelligent, high performer |
| **What Königssee likes:** | Gray mares, new experiences |
| **What Königssee doesn't like:** | Other stallions |
| **Discipline:** | Eventing and dressage |

rival, Franziskus. Therefore, consistent training is extremely important for him, as for all stallions. Especially with stallions, I must pay close attention, making sure I am concentrating on the horse and that my half-halts are more interesting than the environment. Working in a rope halter for groundwork, Königssee also learns to be obedient in his interactions with people. It's not always easy. Especially when there are other horses nearby, he gets worked up easily.

Königssee moves with lots of impulsion and elasticity. Rhythmic and loose, he moves with great balance. When ridden, he grows larger beneath the rider and likes to show off. Supremely confident and self-assured, this "little one" masters all new tasks with ease. He's enjoying a basic training that is full of variety and has been successful in all three disciplines. When the weather is good, we enjoy doing our dressage work in an open field.

During his first competitive season, he gathered many wins and placings in all of the young horse trials where he competed. He was

*A fresh, uphill canter in an open field.*

*Königssee is very well-proportioned.*

Trakehner Champion of the Year in his age group. As a five-year-old, Königssee was successful in dressage, jumping, and cross-country competitions through elementary levels (approximately Second Level dressage and jumps up to 3'9"). He took part in the National Championships for five-year-old event horses. As a six-year-old, he's on the way to Third Level, learning his flying changes easily and with confidence.

## Königssee's Training Plan

As Königssee's basic training was so uncomplicated, we do not need to watch out for anything specific. He should continue to learn and work with ease, maintaining his good attitude, and will otherwise be built up and trained step by step as appropriate to his age.

| SAMPLE WEEKLY TRAINING PLAN | |
|---|---|
| **Monday:** | Free day, out to pasture |
| **Tuesday:** | Dressage-oriented work with cavalletti |
| **Wednesday:** | Hacking out |
| **Thursday:** | Jumping |
| **Friday:** | Dressage, also with work in hand |
| **Saturday:** | Longeing over cavalletti |
| **Sunday:** | Practice a dressage test or stadium course or competition |

# Soma Bay
## — The Likable One

Soma Bay is a very amiable and pretty Westphalian mare, who came to me as a four-year-old directly from her breeder, Leonhard Querdel, and has been in training with me since that time. I was inspired to name her Soma Bay when spending time in Egypt, at a harbor of the same name.

Soma Bay projects a very special magic around her, which no one can resist. Her relaxed and friendly manner and her honest eyes fascinated me immediately. As my father always said, "You must look into the horse's eyes to see if the horse is satisfied and happy. This look, this magic, that's what's most important."

She got comfortable at our place quickly and has only ever shown her best self, so she's got a place in everyone's heart around here. Spontaneously, a friend of mine exclaimed, "She's just so adorable!" When being handled, she is very attentive and polite with her people and enjoys each and every little pat to the absolute fullest.

Physically, she has a very compact, square, and cohesive build, but with lots of neck in front of the rider. She possesses good freedom

*Attentive and sensitive, she always turns an ear to her rider.*

**SOMA BAY**

| | |
|---|---|
| **Nickname:** | Pumba |
| **Breed:** | Westphalian mare by Vitalis/out of Real Diamond |
| **Breeder:** | Leonhard Querdel |
| **Owner:** | FORS |
| **Born:** | 2011 |
| **Character:** | Attentive, tactful, relaxed, friendly, learns easily, adorable |
| **What Soma Bay likes:** | New tasks, praise, being petted, treats, going out to pasture with her pony friends |
| **What Soma Bay doesn't like:** | Actually, Pumba likes everyone and everything |
| **Discipline:** | Dressage |

through her shoulder and a very active hindquarters. Her movement is light and dynamic. From the beginning, I was impressed by her extraordinary rideability. As a three-year-old, she participated in a field test for mares and was awarded a 9.0 for walk, trot, canter, and rideability. The test rider even gave her a 9.5. From all the three-year-old Westphalian riding mares, she had the second best scores and, in addition, won two riding horse tests. As a five-year-old, she placed many times at First Level and, toward the end of the season, won a 9.0 at an aptitude test that included cross-country obstacles with my daughter, Greta, riding. After moving up in dressage to Second Level, she placed second at her first competition.

Soma Bay is very tactful and learns easily. It brings great pleasure to observe how she reacts to the smallest, most sensitive aids, and

*Some Bay is delicate in the hand and her gaits are easy to ride.*

*Pumba likes to jump and gets really round over this oxer.*

especially to my voice. In training, she is always motivated, active, attentive, and keeps both ears on me. From her, I've learned how to scale it back as the rider, communicate very clearly, and really give her my signals using very light aids with lots of feel. Later on with her, I can just think about the exercise I want her to execute.

With unknown exercises, and at competitions, she still stays loose, uncomplicated, and relaxed, while at the same time curious and needing to look at everything around her before she will really concentrate completely on me when under saddle. By nature, this mare possesses a very good, ground-covering walk. Soma Bay likes to jump and is also becoming ambitious cross-country. How much capacity she will have for this in the end is difficult for me to determine right now. Until the end of her sixth year, she'll continue to gather experience in all three disciplines, even though she will probably be primarily a dressage horse.

Soma Bay really enjoys the company of other horses and her favorite way to spend her free time is turned out to pasture with her pony friends. When Carmen goes to retrieve the horses from pasture, Soma Bay does a friendly trot over to Carmen as she enters the field, in order to then allow herself to be led back to the barn, together with the other ponies.

## Soma Bay's Training Plan

Soma Bay will be developed and conditioned step by step as appropriate to her age. As she by nature has such a friendly and positive overall attitude, it is not difficult to direct her enthusiasm toward new tasks. Through training that includes lots of variety, she should have fun and maintain her motivation for work.

**SAMPLE WEEKLY TRAINING PLAN**

**Monday**:
Free day, out to pasture

**Tuesday:**
Gymnasticizing dressage work with cavalletti

**Wednesday:**
Long-lining with Wilfried Gehrmann

**Thursday:**
Longeing over cavalletti

**Friday:**
Galloping in the hills or dressage training out in the open

**Saturday:**
Cavalletti work or gymnastic jumping

**Sunday:**
Hacking or free day out to pasture

# *Dresden Mann*
## — The Superstar

Dresden Mann, nicknamed Alfi, came to our training barn at the end of his fourth year, as a certified stallion from the North Rhine Westphalia rural stud Warendorf. His owner Clodagh Wallace had entrusted the stallion to me for training. He is a chic black stallion, with a cohesive uphill build and a dynamic way of going. From the beginning, he showed a good aptitude for collection and learned new movements playfully. Training him brought me lots of joy, as he was motivated, had lots of energy and was eager to learn. As a four-year-old, he already won a test at Second Level. As a five-year-old, he was the Westphalian Champion, and took sixth place in the World Championships for Young Dressage Horses in Verden. He also made the finals in dressage for five year-olds at the National Championships. At six years old, he was again sixth at the World Champion-

**DRESDEN MANN**

| | |
|---|---|
| Nickname: | Alfi |
| Breed: | Westphalian gelding by Dresemann/ out of Florestan I |
| Breeder: | Hubert Vornholt |
| Owner: | Clodagh and Jason Wallace, Ingrid Klimke |
| Born: | 2004 |
| Character: | Confident, eager, likes to show off |
| What Alfi likes: | Having his withers scratched, drinking from the water hose, ponies |
| What Alfi doesn't like: | Being at the back when ridden out, being cleaned under his belly |
| Discipline: | Dressage |
| Level of Training: | Completely trained dressage horse, through Grand Prix |

*Thanks, Alfi!*

ships for Young Dressage Horses and at the National Championships.

His talent was indisputable, but all too often, being a stallion stood in his way. In such moments, it was only with great difficulty that I got him to concentrate through a test. Even with good training, ground-work, and getting him familiar with lots of stimuli, we could not manage to fix this so that he would be well mannered in his environment and attentive at work. In the dressage arena, he would sometimes buck so hard that I had to assume the defensive seat usually reserved for riding cross-country. Therefore, together with his owners Clodagh and Jason Wallace, we decided to geld him when he was seven. This was the best decision we ever could have made. Since that time, he has developed positively in every regard. He's much more even-tempered, although he remains a self-confident and sometimes dominant horse.

*Dresden Mann piaffes in an open field.*

But now, in a dressage test, he can concentrate on me wholeheartedly and strives to get everything right.

Good riding changes the horse in a positive sense. He gets more beautiful, developing muscles in the right place, getting rounder and more expressive. With Alfi, I can look back over the years and really recognize this development.

As a seven-year-old, Alfi placed at Prix St. Georges, and at eight, he won many tests at high levels. A great success for us was earning third place at the Nurnberger Burgpokal Finals. At nine, he had a phenomenal season. Our move up to Grand Prix went superbly: two starts, two wins at K&K Cup in Munster. With the qualifying win for the Finals at Louisdor Preis and more starts, Alfi got more and more secure in the difficult movements and we even surmounted the 80 percent hurdle in the Kur in Munster in front of the castle. The German Olympic Committee for Riding (DOKR) honored Dresden Mann at the Stuttgarter Schleyerhalle with the Otto-Lörke Prize. The Otto-Lörke Prize is given annually to the rider, trainer, and owner of the dressage horse, maximum 10 years of age, which attracted the attention of the Dressage Committee because of his outstanding performance at Grand Prix Dressage.

At the end of his ninth year, Dresden Mann injured himself and needed a long break. We gave him the time he needed to be ready for work again. This meant six months pasture rest. Afterward, we slowly resumed his training. He had not forgotten a single movement.

Our re-entry to competition happened in Munster at the beginning of his eleventh year. Alfi shone above the rest and was very motivated. He executed each movement, dancing and floating. In Balve at the German Championships, we got better with each test and afterward were again members of the German Equestrian Federation's B-Kader.

It brings me enormous joy to ride Alfi, as he has always given his all for me and presented himself so well and enthusiastically. He was simply a little superstar, who lifted hearts. Unfortunately, during his eleventh year, I had to retire Dresden Mann from dressage for reasons of soundness. After a long pasture rest, we looked for a new job for him.

## Alfi's Training Plan

As Alfi's talent was clearly for dressage, it was the focal point of his training. But, even as a dressage horse, for conditioning purposes Alfi came with us on our adventures and galloping in the hills. On his day off from training, he really enjoyed being ridden bareback and with only a neck ring at times. He liked being ridden over cavalletti and did not shy away from taking a jump or two from time to time. Alfi mastered all exercises through the highest levels. Wilfried Gehrmann supported me with the collected exercises, coming once a week to the barn.

*Alfi fully alert in the hills.*

**SAMPLE WEEKLY TRAINING PLAN**

**Monday**:
Free day, out to pasture

**Tuesday:**
Loosening dressage work, basics with cavalletti

**Wednesday:**
Riding in double bridle, dressage movements with work in hand

**Thursday:**
Riding out (loosening and conditioning)

**Friday:**
Longeing over cavalletti

**Saturday:**
Longeing over cavalletti

**Sunday:**
Competition or gymnastic jumping with cavalletti

# *Abraxxas*
## — The Little Fighter with the Huge Heart

For many years, Abraxxas was my championship horse. With him, I competed twice in eventing at the Olympic Games and won Team Gold. Braxxi has been an extremely special horse for me. In the meantime, he's also become a wonderful schoolmaster for my daughter, Greta. Following Braxxi's retirement from upper-level competition in June of 2014, I wrote a letter to him, explaining what his career and he himself have meant to me. I couldn't describe this any better:

## To Braxxi, on Your Retirement from High-Performance Competition

While I was searching for Sleep Late's successor, Hans and Chris discovered you. Carmen and I saw you for the first time in Luhmühlen: a small, black horse with small pony hooves, and a very refined, efficient way of going. Looking at you with my "dressage hat" on, I was not initially jumping up and down with excitement. Then, over the first

*Braxxi — going cross-country, he was in his element.*

| FRH BUTTS ABRAXXAS | |
| --- | --- |
| **Nickname:** | Braxxi |
| **Breed:** | Hanoverian gelding by Heraldik xx/out of Kronenkranich xx |
| **Breeder:** | Fritz Butt |
| **Owner:** | Madeline Winter-Schulze, Ingrid Klimke |
| **Born:** | 1997 |
| **Character:** | Loyal, clever, sensitive |
| **What Braxxi likes:** | Playing out at pasture with his ponies, jumping for joy, treats |
| **What Braxxi doesn't like:** | Galloping at the back of the group, sugar, flies |

cross-country jump, I already had the sense you would be fast and secure on course. The first jump over colorful poles was not so impressive on that hot, sunny day, but with the hope that we could attend to that, you came to our training barn in 2005.

Carmen still remembers your first days and weeks with us: you seemed to her small and unremarkable, but you quickly taught us and showed us your real character. I was still not sure if your basic quality was enough, but I liked you from the beginning, you small, self-confident pony. It quickly became clear: you wanted to stay. With great performance capability, endurance, heart, and strength of will, you mastered every step of your training with gusto. Along the way, Carmen became your best and most trusted friend — always supporting you, tending to you, and building you up as best as possible. You thanked us for this with your unwavering physical soundness.

From 2007 on, you represented Germany on championship teams for six years straight. In 2008, when we won Team Gold at the Hong Kong Olympics and again in 2012 in London, you fought with me to win gold for the team. This was an incredible performance and the only horse to match this was Charisma with Mark Todd (1984 and 1988).

After Hong Kong, you were to be sold. It was only thanks to Madeline Winter-Schulze, who fortunately purchased you, we were able to stay together.

After our second Team Gold in London, I was already being asked if I would retire you from upper-level competition after this sensational success.

*Braxxi at the Four Star event in Burghley 2013.*

*Great celebration after perfect dressage at the European Championships in 2011.*

*Carmen and Braxxi are a well-practiced team.*

I started the season at Badminton to determine how fit and motivated you were at this point— and you were super. At this point, Escada had shown her championship quality in Malmö, but you pushed through a week later in Burghley and maintained the number one spot. Burghley was one of our most difficult cross-country rides together, and there, you again gave your giant fighting heart to me.

Often I asked myself, when it would be the right time to go easier with you and I hoped you would give me a sign — as Sleep Late did. In this season, you were as fresh and motivated as ever: up until that point there had never been a German horse and rider who finished in the top five at the British Four Star classic at Burghley. There are only five Four Star tests in the whole world, and of those five you have successfully completed four of them — the trip to Australia is something we won't take on together. You simply couldn't have been better!

Dearest Braxxi, the right moment has arrived — it's time to take on new tasks. Carmen, who you are so attached to, and I will continue to train you and keep you fit. You're still our best guy: between hunter paces and hacking, and the children who can learn so much from you, you won't be bored. We'll take great pleasure in your high spirits as we watch you play in the pasture with your two buddies, Nemo and

Barny. In the meantime, you have learned to read and write, according to Carmen, and are always in a good mood and having fun with everyone. When Carmen rides you bareback and with a neck ring, you both experience pure joy. It's living proof of your deep friendship and trust in one another.

We are going to mark your retirement surrounded by your fans in the place where we first saw you and where you had your best placing at a Four Star event, coming in second: Luhmühlen.

Dear Braxxi, I thank you for countless unforgettable moments of pure happiness. To dance with you in the dressage arena — what a feeling of lightness. On the most difficult cross-country courses in the world, you were always "quick as a rabbit" (to quote Chris Bartle) and fought like a lion. So often you moved my heart. You gave me your boundless trust and never doubted I would choose the right path for us. We were a wonderful team and could always rely on one another. Show-jumping is not your strength — often, I was very disappointed. Indeed, every horse that has entered my life has had a lesson for me: from you, I learned one must simply accept certain realities in order to then do better at living with them.

Braxxi, I thank you for that, as I take what I learned from you with me on my path as a person and a rider. Always, I hear my father's voice in my ear, "We want to understand the horse's character, pay attention to his personality, and then not squelch it during his training!" You are a very big horse personality, dearest Braxxi, and you'll always be so for me!

*Braxxi and Greta already have the next cross-country jump in sight.*

*Greta can learn a lot from Professor Braxxi.*

# *Afterword*
## — Last But Not Least

# *Thank You*
## — With My Whole Heart

Thanks to all of the people who contributed to the success of this book. First, I want to thank my family, who always stand behind me and have my back. A giant thank you to Carmen and my team, without whose daily support I could not have the life with horses that I am so fortunate to have. To be honest, the creation of this book was a giant experiment, one I would not have attempted without the tireless support of my editor, Alexandra Haungs. I thank you so much that you kept me motivated to stick with it and didn't give up! A hearty thanks, too, for Horst Streitferdt's amazing photos and the wonderful commitment to photographing. A giant thanks to Carina Bein for your efficient help with photo session and with choosing photos. We all worked together so well as a team.

01

02

03

01 Ingrid and Alexandra with Bobby at a photo session.

02 Carina and Soma Bay are good friends.

03 Horst Streitferdt in action, photographing us over two days.

04 Andreas having lots of fun during the photo session on the hills.

05 As always, Carmen made each horse shine.

06 Traveling with eight horses by truck and trailer.

07 Teamwork to saddle, bridle, and screw in studs.

# INDEX

# THANK YOU TO ALL MY SPONSORS, SUPPORTERS, AND PARTNERS